The Layguide

The Layguide

The Rules of The Game

Tony Clink

HarperCollins*Entertainment*
An Imprint of HarperCollins*Publishers*

HarperCollins*Entertainment*
An Imprint of HarperCollins*Publishers*
77–85 Fulham Palace Road,
Hammersmith, London W6 8JB

www.harpercollins.co.uk

A Paperback Original 2005
1

First published in the USA by
Kensington Publishing Corp. 2004

A catalogue record for this book
is available from the British Library

ISBN 0 00 722136 3

Set in Palatino and Avenir

Printed and bound in Great Britain by
Clays Limited, St Ives PLC

PUA (pick-up artist). An adult male who has mastered the art of seducing, romancing, and fulfilling beautiful women. Characteristics include confidence, good grooming, and a high rate of success in sexual situations. PUAs understand that all situations involving attractive women are sexual situations.

AFC (average frustrated chump). A term coined by Ross Jeffries (www.seduction.com) to describe a healthy, horny adult male who has not put enough thought into what women want and need, and therefore has no chance of ever successfully seducing and fulfilling them. Characteristics include hanging on to abusive relationships, moping over a lack of success, spending hundreds of dollars on fruitless dates, and wasting countless nights on small talk with unattractive women that ultimately goes nowhere.

HB (honey bunny). The most beautiful woman in the room, and the object of every PUA's quest.

Contents

2: THE PICK-UP

4: CLOSING THE DEAL

Disclaimer

*"Always two there are . . . a master . . .
and an apprentice."*
—Yoda

Well, not this time, my friend. I've studied the teachings of the best PUAs on the planet and I've seduced countless women, but that doesn't necessarily make me a master. Even if it does, I just don't have the time or patience to train each one of you as my PUA wingman.

That's why I created this book. I've accumulated the best advice in the world on the art of seduction, and I'd rather spend my time using that knowledge than sharing it with each of you individually. By writing this book, I only have to say it once to tell it to the world.

The other reason I created this book is that, after years of studying the words and actions of master PUAs from around the world, then testing these techniques on the world's most beautiful women (very successfully, of course), I realized I had acquired the proverbial Holy Grail of seduction. I didn't want to lose a single nugget of wisdom, so I decided to write it all down. I have since used this guide as a personal reference tool to refresh my memory, refine my techniques, and give me a boost when I am feeling underconfident. These pages have worked for me, and they're going to work for you, too.

Of course, for legal reasons I can't guarantee anything. The advice in this book is for educational purposes only, and whatever you do with it is solely at your own risk and your own initiative. I will not and cannot accept any responsibility for lovesick female stalkers, sexually transmitted diseases, unwanted children, or any other result of your using the techniques in this book.

I will also not take credit for your having more sex with better looking women than you ever thought possible. The wisdom is here. What you do with it is up to you.

Prologue

Stop for a moment and reflect. What is it you strive for in life? To be famous, only to be forgotten when the next big thing comes along? To have more money than your neighbor? To get a promotion and a slightly bigger office? Why? To win the love and respect of a beautiful woman? To have great sex, whenever you want, with the women of your dreams?

What if you could skip through the struggle and go straight to the prize? Maybe you're in school under a pile of books; maybe you're in a cubicle or office; maybe you're in a bookstore, looking to improve yourself.

Wouldn't you rather be talking with a beautiful woman, making her laugh at your jokes, touching her elbow, and moving in closer and closer until your lips are almost touching?

There are beautiful women everywhere. If you're in a public place, look around. Do you see her? She could be yours. If you're at home, think about your day. It was full of beautiful women—at the coffee shop, the office, the gym, on the street. All those women are having sex, every single one of them *loves* to have sex, and there is absolutely no reason why they shouldn't be having it with you.

It doesn't matter how you look or how much money you have, because seduction isn't about those things. Seduction is about attitude, and the right attitude is something anyone can have. Yes, even you, even if you've never spoken to a woman or had a date in your whole life. And, as you'll soon learn, seducing beautiful women isn't even difficult ... *if* you know the basic principles.

Sure, some people are going to get women the old-fashioned way. They're going to spend years working themselves to the bone, then pump away their evenings in the gym, and in the end they'll become rich or famous. When they do, they'll get the women. The rest of us are going to spend our time working just as hard ... and we'll just barely scrape by. Then, after an exhausting day at the office, we're going to go out there and display our goods (some muscles, a new watch, a few jokes) and hope some woman likes what she sees.

Why don't we just cut to the chase and get girls right here, *right now*, by doing things the right way? Believe me, there is nothing more impressive than having a beautiful woman on your arm. The Rolex watch, the Armani suit, the Mercedes Benz, those are all just tools to get the ultimate status symbol: the woman of your (and every other guy's) dreams.

I've been intimate with hundreds of women, each of whom could make you cry—they are so beautiful and fun to be with. And you know what, I'm not rich or particularly good looking. What's my secret? Easy. While you were working late at the office *hoping* to get a beautiful woman some day, I was using the art of seduction to sleep with the woman of your dreams *today*.

But it didn't have to be me. It could have been you.

For more than a decade, I have read books, talked with friends and strangers, and searched the Internet looking for the best and most interesting ideas on picking up women. I've frequented chat rooms and virtual bulletin boards, and hunted for lone wolves eager to share their techniques. I tried out these tips to determine which ones were duds and which ones really worked, and traded my personal secrets with like-minded players around the world. And, of course, I've had lots and lots of fabulous interaction with women, from steamy one night (or one hour) stands to my current two-year relationship with the most wonderful woman in the world.

No matter what your goal, and no matter what your experience, *The Layguide* will lead you to the place of your dreams. Do you want to have sex with a different beautiful woman every night of the week? This book will show you how. Do you want to play the field in search of that one special woman? This book will show you how to do that, too. Do you already know the woman of your dreams, but are afraid to approach her for fear of rejection? I can't agree with your strategy (a PUA never invests that much emotion in a relationship until he's sampled the goods), but I'll still turn you into a confident, sophisticated lover that simply can't lose.

Unlike other seduction guides, *The Layguide* is strictly no experience required. Even if you've never spoken to a woman in your life, I'll show you step-by-step how to become the confident, successful "lay man" you've always wanted to be. And if you're an experienced seducer, I'll take you to heights of success you never thought possible.

Think of the most beautiful woman you've ever met. Now think of her licking her lips slowly with the tip of her tongue, softly touching your elbow with her fingers, leaning over and blowing seductively in your ear, rubbing against your leg, and begging to come back to your place for the time of her life.

If you want to make that dream a reality, read on.

Introduction:
Falling in Love vs. Being a Player

The question of falling in love is tricky. It's not for everyone. On the other hand, it is for some people, and it just may be for you. This book does not teach you how to fall in love, or how to recognize the signs of so-called "true" love. It is a guide to seducing women. You can use it to have brilliant, meaningless sex with a different gorgeous woman every day of the week. If you want to fall in love, it will give you the opportunity, and it will teach you to do it the right way.

If you develop a PUA mentality, which you will if you follow the advice in this book, you will be almost immune from developing the pathetic and desperate fixations commonly associated with falling in love, even when you choose to be monogamous. The typical negative effects (jealousy, neediness, depression, etc.) will be far less severe. Your new attitude won't allow these traits to develop, and your lifestyle won't give them enough time to reach their full destructive potential.

If, on the other hand, you want to be a player (at least at first), the word "polyamorous" is probably the closest match to describing how you will operate in love. A player loves.... but many women at once. Being in love with one girl at a time, especially if it is a one-sided feeling, has you fixated. You're giving off vibes of desperation, paralyzing your ability to think clearly and causing you to feel constant fear of being rejected. When your feelings aren't returned, or if they are returned but not exactly the way you were expecting, it lowers your self-esteem, repelling girls even further away in a self-reinforcing downward cycle.

Being in love with many girls at a time (or at least interested in many women at a time, if they've not yet given you cause to reward them with your love) lets you keep thinking coherently and confidently. You acknowledge and understand that there are countless wonderful women, and you are therefore relaxed enough to guide their feelings for you. Your confidence and cool-ness attract girls, forming another cycle of feelings, but this time a *positive* self-reinforcing cycle.

Some say that the ideal is still a one-on-one relationship full of complete and unconditional love. I agree with the latter part of the assertion: complete and unconditional love truly is an ideal. But I have to disagree with the assertion that a one-on-one situation is always better. Sure, every family needs both a mother and a father to raise the children and to support them financially. Should one of the parents go astray, the family could be broken. But does this mean that to protect the integrity of families, *all* relationships should be strictly one-on-one? That no poly-amorous relations are to be allowed to anyone in any situation?

Of course not. We are not role models for other people's chil-dren. As adults, we are free to choose our own course, and what you do in your personal life will not have an effect on society as a whole. You are just not that important, and neither am I.

The other argument for the superiority of monogamous rela-tionships is that the exclusivity of someone's affection gives added value to that affection. The truth is that, yes, exclusivity will bring added value . . . for a while. But soon, this added value will subside into routine. It will be taken for granted, and it will eventually degenerate into boredom. On the other hand, non-exclusivity can keep things fresh and hot for a very long time indeed.

One last argument promoting the one-on-one relationship is that love is by nature exclusive, and you cannot be in love with two different people at a time. This is a truly weak argument that can only derive from people's lack of experience, or their denial or inability to understand their true feelings. But sooner or later, even the most frigid moralists have to acknowledge the possibility of being able to share love with several people, at least to some degree. Do they love their parents just one at a time? Do they plan on loving their children one at a time? Of course not. They feel love for all of them. Maybe more for some and less for others, but definitely not "only one at a time." Some might argue that sexual love is "different," but I'd say it is only a matter of degrees. Love is love. Period.

Too often, monogamy isn't about love. In fact, a one-on-one relationship is usually more a matter of comfort and tradition than passion. After years of fruitless pursuits and painful rejections, you've finally found someone you like and someone who likes you back, a companion, with whom you can have your need to give and receive love fulfilled. You sigh a sigh of relief and settle in. You're an AFC headed for marriage.

I want to stress, of course, that there's nothing wrong with monogamous relationships, falling in love, or getting married. I encourage you to pursue your own brand of love and relationships and, no matter what your ideal, this book will take you to where you truly want to go.

My concern is that, too often, people "fall in love" because they don't think they have a choice in the matter. When it turns out they could have actually had a choice and there were even better options available, they close their eyes and start preaching about the benefits and superiority of their way of life.

This book is about choices. It is about giving you all the wisdom you need to explore every avenue before deciding which path is right for you. So either seduce to your heart's content, or fall in love and get married, or even become a monk and lead a life of celibacy. Just be sure that, whatever choice you make, you make it with full knowledge and your eyes wide open to *all* of your options.

PART

Getting Started

CHAPTER 1

The Ten Rules of Seduction

Rule #1: Always Be in Control

People ask me all the time: Tony, what's the most important aspect of being a successful seduction artist? What's the one crucial difference between a masturbation-addicted AFC and a sexually satisfied PUA?

The answer to that question is simple: control. PUAs are always in control. AFCs let something else—the woman, another man, their emotions—dictate how they're going to act and what they're going to get in the end.

If you want to be successful with the women, the first thing you must control is yourself. You can never allow yourself to get nervous or panic in a seduction situation. You must remain calm and confident at all times—and you must always exude calm confidence to those around you. Never put too much pressure on yourself, never worry about being rejected, and never, as the old saying goes, let them see you sweat.

The second thing you must control is the situation. A seduction must take place on your terms, and that means you should always be the one to approach the woman, and you should always take the lead in conversation. Act quickly and know exactly what you want, and you'll be on your way to seduction success.

The third thing you must control is the woman. But for God's sake, don't bully or act macho. Control is about subtly leading the woman to where you want her to be (horny and totally into you), and then keeping her there. Women want a man who is confident and powerful. Show her you are a dominant male, and she will instinctively follow where you lead. But remember: With power comes responsibility. Always listen and show her respect. And if you promise her the time of her life, you better make good on that promise.

The fourth thing you must control is the relationship. Never buy a woman drinks or pay for her dinner, except as a reward for sex she has already given you. Never let her break a date or treat you poorly. Always let her know that you are prepared to walk away, and she will be the one that comes crawling to you every time.

Easier said than done, right? Well, if that's your attitude, you're already a chump. Control is easy to achieve because it's entirely in your hands. You already have the power; as long as you have the right attitude, the right techniques, and the right guide (like this book), you can't lose.

Rule #2: Be the Alpha Male

If you watch PBS or the Discovery Channel, you're aware of the concept of the alpha male. The alpha male is the leader of the pack, the acknowledged master of all the rest of the animals in his group. He's the one the women flock to and the men respect. He's the one getting laid all the time, while all the other chumps are wandering around waiting for him to disappear so that they can have their turns. Fat chance, unless one of them becomes the next leader himself, in which case we're back to square one—you still need to be the alpha male.

Now watch those nature shows closer, and you'll realize something very important: the alpha male isn't necessarily the strongest or the best-looking member of the group. *The alpha male is simply the guy that gets laid.* Why do women want him? Because he's the alpha male, of course. It's a self-fulfilling prophecy: Project the image of the alpha male and women will flock to you. Because you're laying all the women, you are by definition the alpha male. The first step is the hard part; after that, it only gets easier—and better.

In other words, all you have to do is show a woman you're a dominant man, and she'll be on her knees for you . . . literally.

The secret is this: women instinctively love a powerful man. The keyword, of course, is instinctively. Even the very hottest woman, the one with all the attitude, the one who seems so proud and in charge, wants to surrender herself (at least for one night) to the man with the sexual power. Her attitude is merely a front to weed out all the submissive males; she doesn't want someone weaker than her, she wants someone who can stand up and give to her as good as he gets. She may dominate the conversation, and dominate you in bed (and I'm all for that!), but she still wants to respect you in the morning.

So what is the first step to becoming a dominant male? How do you become a "lay guy" without first getting laid? Easy. You simply have to project the image of the alpha male. You do this not by getting muscles and money, but by changing your attitude. When you believe you're an alpha male, you believe that women should want to be with you. When you project that image, guess what? Women will want to be with you.

The catch is that *you can't fake it*. You really have to believe you are the best man for this girl. Transform yourself, and you will transform your reality. Doubt yourself, and you set yourself up for failure.

The easiest way to transform yourself from a submissive loser into a winner is to determine what the model of an alpha male should be . . . then become that model. Again, this has nothing to do with strength, looks, or money, so don't picture yourself any different physically. Instead, picture yourself as:

- Confident, because you know you're an alpha male.
- Outgoing, because you know women want to be with you.
- Well-groomed, because you know people are watching you.
- Attentive, because you know your status is based on pleasing the ladies.
- Authoritative, because you're in control of the situation.
- Fun to be around, because you know that, in the end, the woman is going to choose you over the submissive male, even if the submissive male is chatting her up and buying her drinks.

I'll go into all these traits in more detail later, but right now I want to touch on one last point, and this may be the best thing of all. In human communities, there is more than one alpha male. Unlike a group of lions or seals, we're not fighting over eight or ten females; we've literally got millions of women to choose from. That means you don't have to worry about a pumped up muscle boy or a smooth operator encroaching on your territory. You don't have to be the biggest stud in the room, and you *never* have to fight to prove you're a man. All you have do to get laid is stand out from the pathetic crowd, and that's not so hard, right?

A good PUA doesn't worry about the other dominant males; we're all in this together, boys, so let's all have some fun. It's the women we've got to keep our eyes on.

Rule #3: Look Your Best . . . Always

To meet women, you must be prepared, both physically and emotionally. You need to feel great about yourself, and I don't just mean confident, I mean *great*. And the first step to feeling great about yourself is looking great . . . all the time.

AFCs have an appearance problem. They worry about the fact that they're short, bald, overweight, and acne scarred—and they let that affect things like their posture, their facial expression, and their body language. If I've said it once, I've said it a million times: looks don't matter. It's not the bald head that turns women off, it's the lack of confidence that bald head creates in the man.

What matters is the way you feel about yourself, because women are going to pick up on your attitude and echo it back to you. If you approach a woman with the attitude that you're not good looking enough for her, you'll convince her it's true. If you project the image that you're plenty good-looking and she's lucky to get the opportunity to be with you, you'll win her over . . . even if she is skeptical at first.

Never worry about the things you can't change (and no, nose jobs don't count). Always pay attention to the things you can change. Your clothes should always be clean and fit properly. Your hair should always be styled. Your teeth should always be brushed, as fresh breath is very important, and, of course, you should always be clean and showered. Never take a trip for granted, even if it's just down to the corner store for a six-pack of beer. As you'll learn later in this book, people meet in the strangest places, and the most accidental encounter may lead to your most rewarding relationship—*if* you're prepared to seize the opportunity.

There's no right or wrong way to dress to impress, but the clothes you wear send a clear message about who you are, so be careful. An Armani suit is nice, but it gives women the impression you're a big spender who's going to buy things for them (which you're not!). A hip, cutting edge look makes you stand out, but some women won't take you seriously, or may feel that you're just not their type because you're making them feel square and affecting their confidence.

A classic "swinger" look, with big gold chains and an open collar, is the worst mistake of all. No woman wants to be played, so never advertise through your dress that you're a player. That shuts the door before you even get started. And for God's sake, never consult this book in front of a woman. Girls don't want something canned and rehearsed, they want something spontaneous (or that at least feels spontaneous). That's why pick-up lines never work.

Do My Looks Matter?

Yes, but not as much as you think. Men judge women primarily on their looks—face, hair, eyes . . . okay, I know, some of you prefer to start this list with tits and ass. More than anything else, though, it is looks that turn us on . . . and turn us off. So it is only natural that we think the same thing holds true for women.

But we're wrong. Women attribute much less importance to how a man looks. What matters to women is *how a man makes them feel*. This is the entire basis of being a PUA, and I can assure you it is true. Good looks—the right face, the right body, the right clothes—will help get you an audition with a woman. But *only* an audition. It's the ability to make the women feel sparkles, tingles, and magic deep down inside that ultimately makes them want to be with you—not your looks.

If you really don't have a style of your own, your best bet is "stylish casual." Upgrade your khaki slacks to some designer black pants. Throw out your golf shirt in favor of a nice button-down. Go for a stylish conservative haircut from a reputable hair stylist, not a barber. This outfit may not open many doors, but it's not going to get them slammed in your face, either.

Remember, it's not the clothes that make the man; it's how you wear them.

Cologne

There are a lot of different opinions on top colognes, but here are a few that I've found get the best results:

- Gucci Nobile
- Armani (not Acqua di Gio)

- Fahrenheit by Christian Dior
- Aqua by Hugo Boss
- Black Jeans by Versace
- Fuck Oil by Dusty

Many people will probably disagree with my choices, and that's fine. But there is one point all successful seduction artists will agree on: wearing cologne matters.

Just think of the effect a woman's seductive perfume has on you. Now imagine how much of an impact your cologne or aftershave is going to have on them. Remember that, in general, women are a lot more sensitive to smell then men. And, unlike women, most men don't wear aftershave or cologne, so the impact of your decision is going to stand out that much more. In effect, all those chumps going *au naturel* have ceded you this important advantage.

The trick is to buy a cologne or aftershave that is well-known. This can work to your advantage in two specific ways:

1. If you are wearing the scent her father usually wears, it will strongly work in your favor.
2. Women love to guess the kind of cologne you're wearing. This gives you a great opening to discuss something that puts them on comfortable ground: cosmetics. If they can correctly guess the fragrance you're wearing, that goes one step further and gives you an instant point of common ground.

The primary point here, though, is not to tell you which cologne to wear. That is up to you. The point is that, if you're not thinking long and hard about the cologne you're wearing and its effect on your intended prey, you're not putting enough care and attention into your personal appearance. In seduction, as in all other arts, it's the little things that make the difference.

Rule #4: Be Confident

Confidence is the most important trait for an alpha male to develop. Confidence means that you feel comfortable approaching any woman at any time, because even before you meet her, you know that you are the perfect experience for her. Alpha males never wonder if they're good enough for the woman; they wonder if the woman is good enough for them. They never offer anything to a woman. They're not trying to sell themselves; they're trying to find out what the woman has to offer.

Now that you know about confidence . . . forget completely that you've ever heard the word. If you are thinking about feeling confident, then you're not really confident; you're nervous and unsure of yourself. If you're truly an alpha male, you'll feel so positive about a sexual encounter that the word "confidence" will never cross your mind. Feeling so good and natural that you never have to think about confidence is the most confident act of all. Concentrate on feeling relaxed and positive, and you'll project an air of confidence to the woman every time.

If you need a little boost to approach a beautiful woman, do not tell yourself to be confident, be confident, be confident. Instead, repeat this mantra: "I am the best thing that has ever happened to that girl. I am the perfect experience for that girl." Now think of the way she will have goosebumps because of the way you make her feel inside and, if you want, imagine for a split second all the ways you can make her cum. Don't dwell on that, though. Just go and offer her the experience of a lifetime!

Rule #5: Always Have the Right Mind-set

If you've been to a club, you've seen those guys standing or sitting on the side of the dance floor, looking at the girls but not making a move, waiting for something to happen. Their mind-set is, "If I stand around long enough, maybe something will happen." They make me want to laugh. That herd of chumps is known as "death row," and I don't have to tell you that death row is not the place you want to be.

So, why are you standing there on death row like a pathetic clown? I'm not just talking about at the night club, I'm talking about in everyday life. Are you even noticing all those beautiful women that you pass every day? Are you making eye contact? Are you trying to do something more than stare at their asses when they're not looking, or looking away as soon as they glance in your direction? Some guys call this being oblivious, some guys call it being scared, but either way, you're on death row. If you're not taking advantage of the fact that you are surrounded every minute of the day by beautiful women, then you're no better than those chumps alongside the dance floor. Like them, you're going home alone, remembering all the beautiful girls you saw, and sleeping with your hand.

If you're in a club, the obvious answer is to hit the dance floor. The same is true in the real world. Before you head out that door, remind yourself that you are about to meet a beautiful woman—so be prepared to do something more than stare at her ass while hoping you don't get caught.

Rule # 6: Worship the Three Second Rule

There is one rule you must always remember, and in all honesty, this may be the most important thing I'll teach you. It's an old PUA secret called the Three Second Rule, or simply 3S.

3S is this: Once you spot a girl, you have three seconds—and three seconds only—to make your move. If you hesitate . . . forget it. Put her behind you and move on to the next available female.

Even if you cannot think of anything to initiate the conversation, do not break the Three Second Rule. You've got to get noticed out there, and you've got to give that girl a good first impression. When you use 3S—no, *worship* 3S—you are showing her that you are fearless. You are taking the initiative and staking out the high ground, and that can only work in your favor.

If you don't worship 3S, you are in a decidedly weaker position. First, you're not going to appear spontaneous or strong. Instead, if you're making a lot of eye contact or just obviously hesitating, you're going to appear weak and unsure of yourself. Instead of talking with her, you're giving that woman time to form an opinion of you, and that opinion is that you're just like all the others: afraid to make your move.

Meanwhile, you're not doing yourself any favors by waiting. When you hesitate, you're just giving yourself time to get intimidated and start inventing excuses about why you shouldn't approach this woman.

That's the other advantage to 3S: it doesn't give you the opportunity to overthink the situation. You have no time to become sweaty, trembling, stuttering—in other words, to acquire all the signs of a classic AFC. Granted, if you're new to this, or if the woman is really attractive, you might start stuttering and sweating during the conversation, but at least you will already have your foot in the door. You made a good first impression—and that's going to stick with her long after the sweat on your hands has dried. Besides, if you get off on the right foot, you're much less likely to turn into a bowl of jelly during the conversation.

And don't worry, once you've used 3S a few times, you'll learn to think up a great opener in the time it takes to walk up to her.

Rule #7: Never Be a Nice Guy

The debate over being a nice guy or a jerk is one of the oldest struggles in the sexual universe. Nice guys are considerate, polite, friendly, tender, attentive, and romantic. They tend to have lots of female friends but not a lot of female lovers, and they can spend a whole night talking with a beautiful woman, only to have her slip away on the arm of some "jerk" the minute they go to the bathroom.

Let's face it, jerks get the women. Because of that, most people assume that a book of seduction advice (like this book) will teach men to be jerks. You know what? That's entirely true.

The problem is that most people—or I should say *all* people who don't understand the rules of the game—have the definitions of "nice guys" and "jerks" all wrong. They think a jerk is an overconfident, aggressive, impolite, self-obsessed, sexually charged muscle boy who doesn't care the least about the women he sleeps with. That's not true at all . . . but even I have to admit that nine times out of ten the guy I just described will be the one shagging the girl upstairs, while the nice guy is left standing outside in the rain with a fistful of wilted flowers.

Why? It's not because women like jerks. Women prefer polite over rude, and attentive over distracted. The problem is the way nice guys present these positive characteristics. In order to appear friendly and romantic, these "nice guys" think they have to turn off their sexuality. They hide their desires in order not to offend, presenting an androgynous, asexual persona. The first impression they give is one of emasculation, weakness, and lack of desire. At best, they confuse the woman as to whether they even find her attractive. At worst, she totally loses respect for them. Do I even need to tell you that this is a huge mistake?

Women want to know you want them: it sets them on sure footing and clears up any apprehensions of not having their desires returned. In order to make this clear, you have to embrace your sexual feelings and become comfortable with sexual issues. Is it wrong to let a woman know you find her very attractive and stimulating? Is it rude to be honest about the fact that, like everyone else on the planet, you enjoy sex?

That's what jerks offer women that nice guys don't: they're not afraid to be sexual. It is the sexual charge that attracts the women, because women are sexual beings, too—and they want to be with someone confident enough to please their every desire.

So, go ahead and be polite, attentive, romantic, and considerate—those are all traits that you will learn to use and embrace in this book. But never, ever forget to let her know you want to get it on.

A PUA is considered a jerk by two types of people: the men whose women he steals, and the women who think he lied and treated them like dirt. Forget the men. Those guys are losers. But always watch your reputation with the women. Never lie to a woman. If you're after a one-night stand, let her know that *very* clearly. If you're seeing multiple women, tip her off *before* she climbs in your bed. And if you tell a woman you're going to call her, *always* call her. No exceptions.

Rule #8: Never Go on a Date

Some of you may be out there thinking: Wow, wouldn't it be great to go on a date with a beautiful woman, a woman who respects me, who wants me, who can't take her eyes off me . . .

Well, think again, chump. If you're going to be a successful PUA, or even just get the woman of your dreams, lose that image of the romantic, candle-lit dinner . . . at least for the fore-seeable future. There are a zillion better ways to get to know a girl: do sports together, rent a movie, meet for a cup of coffee.

What's the worst thing you can possibly do with a woman?

Offer to buy her a drink. You've just sent every wrong message possible: desperation, free spending, lack of power, not to mention it's the worst cliché in the book. If I say it once, I'm going to say it a thousand times: never put out a dollar for a woman until she's put out for you.

Just never call it a "date," and always make sure she pays for her own food and drink. If she refuses to pay, eject her; she was only interested in the free ride anyway. Are you the kind of guy who pays for sex? I don't think so.

Is there ever an appropriate time to go on a date with a woman? Actually, yes. Dates are the exclusive privilege and reward for women you are already sleeping with. Period. End of story.

Rule #9: Learn to Love Rejection

"The difference between winners and losers is that losers don't fail enough."

—Ross Jeffries (www.seduction.com)

The truth is that, once you've read and mastered the advice in this book, you will never be rejected. Why? Because you'll never use a lousy pick-up line, ask for a dance out of the blue, or give her any other opportunity to reject you first thing. And once you're in the pilot's seat, you'll know how to read the signs and self-eject before she shoots you down, if, in fact, that's where she's headed.

However, in the early days, and even sometimes later in your development, you will get rejected. Don't take it personally. Just because she doesn't want you now, doesn't mean she won't want you in the future. Maybe you didn't try hard enough. Maybe your approach was wrong. Maybe she was in a bad mood. Maybe she has a boyfriend, so she cut you off before you could convince her to cheat on him.

Maybe she'll come around later, either in a few hours or on a different evening. If she doesn't, who cares? After all, she's the one missing out on a great experience. You were about to give her a fantastic gift and she turned it down, poor girl.

*"I never get rejected. I only discover if a
woman has good taste!"*

—Ross Jeffries (www.seduction.com)

The fact is, even the best PUAs lose more times than they score. Can you imagine batting .500? That would mean that every time you approached two women, one of them would end up sleeping with you! Believe me, it's not going to happen. You may bat .500 for a week, a month, or even a summer, but ultimately that pace is too much to sustain.

The key to being a successful PUA is to be able to handle rejection. You can't let one bad encounter get you flustered or destroy your confidence. Instead, think of rejection as a positive. Every time you get rejected, you learn something. In other words, every time a woman turns you down, you're that much closer to getting laid.

Johnny Shack's Three Reasons for Rejection

According to PUA Johnny Shack, there are only three reasons a woman will reject you:

1. The boyfriend (if she's a monogamous woman, that's no reflection on you).
2. She wants your PUA wingman (he's a PUA—so there's no shame there).
3. She isn't confident enough to say yes. Believe it or not, many women automatically reject men because they don't feel good enough about themselves to say yes (The problem is *hers*, not yours, so move on.).

Is he right? Who cares! Remember these three points, and they will help you keep your confidence every time. Remember: *She's* the one missing out.

After all, you can't get a hit if you don't step up to the plate, so keep trying and never attach too much importance to winning and losing. Never get too high if a woman accepts your advances. It's just sex, and one great encounter doesn't mean you're a winner for life. Never get too low when a woman turns you down. You're not a loser because some woman won't sleep with you—she's the one losing out.

Don't get me wrong. Rejection isn't easy. For most people, it's the hardest part of the transition from AFC to PUA. That's why the next section is filled with practical advice on learning to let the insults roll off your back and out of your mind. Because when you can handle rejection, everything else will fall into place: your confidence, mind-set, and attitude.

When you can handle rejection with style and class, you become an alpha male.

Rule #10: There's Always Another Woman

I know that a lot of you probably bought this book so that you could finally start a conversation with that beautiful dream girl you see every day down at the coffee shop. Well, I've got news for you: you're never going to get her. At least not that way.

The problem is that you've got exactly the wrong attitude. If some woman is your only prospect, the one you're thinking of day and night, playing out different scenarios of approaching her and making her like you—that's called desperation. And it will show. She's going to see it, consciously or unconsciously, and nothing repels girls more than a desperate guy.

When you let yourself fall into the obsession trap, you begin to overanalyze everything your dream girl does, every move she makes, everything she says . . . and then you relate it all back to yourself. The result? Confusion, frustration, and anxiety. There goes your confidence, and there goes any chance you had of giving her a positive, comfortable projection of yourself.

Yes, your obsession will drive you crazy, but the effect you're having on her is even worse. If she senses you're obsessed with her, she will know you've been analyzing her every move. At best, this will make her self-conscious around you. At worst, you're really going to creep her out, and she's going to go out of her way to avoid you.

But, wait. Maybe she shares the attraction. Maybe by showing her you're obsessed with her, but not man enough to approach her, she'll give you a positive sign that will take the pressure off and guarantee your success. If you're obvious enough, maybe she'll even approach you first!

Are you listening to yourself? That's pathetic. First, never leave the ball in the woman's court. You've got to be in control of the situation, or you have no chance of success. That's PUA rule number one.

Second, if she gives you a signal, will you even know it? More likely, you'll miss the signal, or doubt that the signal is real, and once again talk yourself out of approaching her.

If you're obsessed with a woman, if you want her so much that you can't handle the thought of rejection (a definite PUA no-no), there's only one thing you can do: make love to at least ten other women. Once you do that, you'll ease up on the obsession and feel more relaxed around her. If this is your first love, or if she's the reason you bought this book, then make love to at least twenty women. That will give you the confidence you need to approach your dream girl the right way, with the right attitude. And remember, when it comes to women, confidence is everything.

And, who knows? After making passionate love to twenty other women, maybe you'll realize she isn't the only woman you want in this life after all. If she's still your dream girl, then congratulations. With my advice and your experience, she will be yours.

But first, of course, you have to pick up at least twenty other women. So we better get started learning how to meet ladies.

And Remember . . .

You are a traveling salesman, giving women only a foretaste of the goods and offering them an opportunity to get the real stuff . . . *if* they play their cards right. AFCs consider women "goods" which they try to win and eventually date, purchasing them with movies, dinners, and gifts. In fact, *you* are the goods, but you're not selling yourself to everyone—you are on offer only to a select group of potential customers. You don't need to push it or "sell" it. The stuff is real and you know it, and if the customer doesn't want it, it's her loss—another one will gladly grab you up.

But don't forget, nobody will want your goods if they don't know anything about them. So give them a sample by demonstrating value and personality. But only a sample! You are high-class product, and you don't come cheap.

CHAPTER **2**

Getting Started
with Women

The Truth About Women

The first myth about women is that they have to be totally into you, to really want you badly, to go out with you. That's obviously a pretty high bar to hurdle, but the good news is that it's totally false. In fact, a woman will usually accept your advances (but not necessarily put out) as long as she finds you relatively attractive and, most importantly, interesting.

Most single women are lonely. That's a fact. Guys often approach women and *intend* to ask them out, but for some reason don't have the nerve to go through with it. This is especially true with very attractive women, and again I'd like to thank all the AFC's out there for making these women so desperate for a real man that doesn't fear their beauty. When an alpha male (you) actually has the balls to ask these women out for a romantic evening, most women will accept, even if you're not her knight in shining armor (yet).

The second myth is that women aren't looking for guys . . . or sex. Of course they are! Women love romance. They want someone to kiss and hold and go to the movies with. They long to be swept off their feet.

But they're cautious, too, which is why you can never let the first impression blow you off course. Many women intentionally make themselves seem unapproachable, giving off a "leave me alone or I'll bite your head off" vibe as a form of protection against a broken heart. It's also the perfect way to weed out all the supplicating AFCs who don't have a clue how to approach women and are scared off even by the simplest of challenges.

Don't worry. In most cases, this attitude is just a thin shield. If you approach her with confidence, and refuse to take no for an answer, your persistence will pay off. Always remember that getting in the door is the most important part of any seduction, and that behind that hard wall is often a soft romantic heart. Break through the barrier, and you are halfway to the finish line.

The key to crossing that line is to turn her thoughts toward sex. In a good seduction, your innocent conversation will slowly steer her toward thinking of you as a possible mate, instead of just a nice guy. You are planting that idea in her head and are getting her to think about you in a new way. Have you ever had a woman show interest in you, and then suddenly you like her more than you did before? Well, that's essentially what you're doing in a seduction. When you put yourself into her thoughts, and her thoughts are turned toward sex, you're giving yourself a chance!

The object of a seduction is not to take the woman directly to bed. This will happen—and I'll teach you how to spot these women—but in most cases, you'll close the encounter by getting a phone number.

Making a timely exit is a major part of keeping the fish on the hook, but there's also another factor in play: going out on a "date" (we'll talk about the date concept in more detail later) with a stranger is very exciting. The "anything can happen" atmosphere helps to alter a woman's mood. It makes her feel like she's throwing caution to the wind—and makes her susceptible to doing things she normally wouldn't do.

The Hottest Women, and Only the Hottest Women

No matter what the circumstance, and no matter how new you are to the seduction scene, always approach the most attractive women available in the area. This is a hard-and-fast rule that should never be broken. You can always work your way down the list, but are you ever going to pick up a beautiful woman after striking out with an ugly one? I don't think so.

This may sound intimidating—as in, why would a beautiful woman want to be with me?—but stop and think. What do you expect to achieve by approaching that lesser beauty? Do you think she's going to be more receptive because fewer people approach her? Do you think she's going to accept your advances simply out of desperation? Or is this all about you and your comfort level?

No matter what your reasoning, I can assure you that you've got it all wrong. First of all, you're good enough for any woman out there, and if you don't believe that, just head back to the bedroom right now and enjoy your hand. It's not about looks. It's not about money. You're the man that can give her what she wants: a good time.

Second, attractive women aren't any harder to pick up than ugly women. The fact is, *all* women love romance and want to feel special, and very few women are satisfied with what they're getting. Beautiful women often get a lot of attention, but they're rarely asked out because they tend to intimidate the guys.

In other words, if she seems unapproachable . . . then everybody else probably feels the same way, so she's probably alone. That's your opportunity calling.

Talk to Girls . . . Everywhere

You're new at this, you're a little intimidated by beautiful women, but that's okay. No one goes from AFC to PUA overnight. You've got to evolve, like that first fish that stepped out of the water and started breathing that sweet air of freedom.

The most important thing that will take you from sweaty, stuttering AFC to confident, sophisticated PUA is experience. I can tell you a hundred important rules, and give you a thousand tips, but it all comes down to intuition. And you get intuition by . . . you guessed it, actually interacting with women.

If you're going to be a ladies' man, you need to develop confidence in yourself and an intuitive sense for what a woman is feeling. You do this by talking with women *all the time* and everywhere—park, bus, McDonald's, supermarket, carwash, bowling alley, airport, laundromat. Everywhere you go, there are beautiful women, and every time you see one, you must be ready and able to make your move. In fact, until you're an experienced PUA with all kinds of numbers on hand, you should be talking to a minimum of fifty new women every week. And remember, that's a minimum!

Of course, if you're going from zero to fifty, the transition might be a little hard, so go ahead and set aside a few hours in the evenings or a Saturday afternoon dedicated entirely to talking with every beautiful woman you see. And yes, when I say every woman, I mean *every* woman, no matter how intimidating she looks or how awkward the situation. If you don't push yourself, you're never going to learn—and you're never going to get laid.

Need a little more hand-holding? Don't worry, I'll take you step-by-step from hapless virgin to experienced seducer (or at least conversationalist) at the end of the chapter, but right now let's go over a few very important basics.

Capitalize

Sometimes a woman will become interested in you just because you're a smart, well-adjusted, confident alpha male. It could be a co-worker, a neighbor, a fellow student, the check-out girl from your favorite sandwich shop. It happens—all the time.

Signs of Interest

I don't believe in signs of interest. If a woman isn't interested in you right now, that just means you have some work to do to make her interested in you later. The only thing that really matters is whether you're interested in her. Still, I understand this attitude takes a while to develop. So, for all you beginners, here's a cheat sheet on reading a woman across the room, developed from a list by Don Steele:

I'm Interested	Don't Bother
Looks at you out of the corner of her eye	Doesn't sneak a glance
Repeated glances	Quick eye contact
Looks into your eyes quickly	Quickly looks away
Looks away after glancing down	Looks away with her eyes level
Perks up	Posture does not change
Touches hair or clothing	Makes no adjustments
Adjusts body toward you	Moves her body away from you
Changes the angle of her head	Head remains level
Narrows eyes slightly	Eyes are unchanged
Smiles	Does not smile
Mimics your posture	No mimicking posture
Sparkle in her eyes	Eyes unchanged
Licks her lips	No sign of the tongue
Pushes breasts forward	Shoulders sag

If you've got any feelings from her at all, do not let that window of opportunity close! She already likes you, so why let the chance slip through your fingers? Any minute now, a new

Chump File: The Myth of "The Right Time"

Here's a piece of anonymous advice I read recently in an internet chat room:

> Don't rush things sexually with single women . . . If the mood, the time, the place isn't right, or if it feels the slightest bit awkward, don't risk trying to kiss her for the first time. If she's interested, the time and the place will come.

Puh-lease. It takes far less time to become a seasoned PUA than to wait until "the time is right." The whole point of seduction is to work the woman up into a sexual frenzy, until she practically wants to rape you right there on the spot. You're not working on her clock, you're working on your clock, and your clock says the time is right—right now.

Never send mixed messages about your intentions. You don't want to seem too eager, but the end result you desire should never be in doubt.

You're a man. You have sexual desires. There's no point in denying them. Which is exactly the attitude you need to have. Your mantra is, "I am a man. I make no excuses for my desires. I laugh at the hypocrisy of the prude!" If some girl wrinkles up her nose at this, you'll just have to try that much harder to convert her. In the end, she won't understand how she could ever have wanted otherwise.

prospect could catch her eye. Even without the threat of competition (who could compare to you?), her interest could wear off for no discernible reason. So end her suffering and extend a helping hand.

But be careful not to do it in a supplicating, awkward AFC way. That's the primary reason for the "I was interested in him until he became interested in me" phenomenon. Stay on top of your game. Be confident. A girl that has developed an interest in you independently is no different from a girl you just met. You've still got to make her realize you're the man of her dreams by using the techniques in this book. And, if she's interested already, you'd better do it right now!

Do not wait for some nonexistent "right time" to approach her. And never wait for her to make the first move—because she won't. She'll just end up thinking you're not interested or, even worse, some chump too cowardly to go after what you want.

But what if she's not really interested? What if her signs of interest are just random friendliness or your imagination? Now you're thinking like an AFC, fool! Never dismiss a woman's signs of interest or try to talk yourself out of approaching her. Believe me, if you've noticed the signs, they're for real.

Where to Meet Girls

You're a beginner, but you're eager. You've got your house in order, your appearance is impeccable, and your confidence is high. You're an alpha male on the prowl, and you're ready to worship 3S and get right into the thick of the action. Now all you need is some women, so it's time to hit the nearest bar or club and . . .

Not so fast, Romeo. There are much better places to meet women than in the high pressure, high volume, high alcohol world of the dance floor. No matter your level of skill or comfort— and *especially* if you're a beginner—the following options are far easier on your wallet and your confidence than the bar scene.

Shopping malls. Malls are by far the best place to meet women, bar none. For one thing, beautiful women are everywhere. For another, they are usually in motion, so you can extricate yourself easily from an awkward situation—without having to stare at the woman who gave you the brush off for the next few hours. This can be very important to an amateur PUA not yet schooled in the art of handling and deflecting rejection.

Check the stores for attractive clerks or shoppers. The products on the shelves will give you a perfect opener, especially if she's working. After all, it's her job to talk to you about them. If the mall is near an office complex, hit the food court during lunch hour. The place will be packed with women from the offices, many of them lonely for some companionship.

Coffee shops. They're like visiting a bar, but without the alcohol, loud music, and pick-up scene vibe. Before work, at lunch, and in the afternoon these places are packed with women, and this offers you the perfect opportunity to sit down next to one and start a conversation.

Libraries. If there is one place that girls always outnumber guys, it's the library. It's also the last place a woman expects to be picked up, so it's easy to catch them off guard. Before they know what hit them, they'll be ready to take a break from all those boring books.

Self-improvement seminars. These classes are loaded with beautiful, *suggestible* women looking to have their mind expanded by new experiences and advice. And the best part is, you don't even have to sign up. Just find out where they're being held, and wait outside the door until it's time for the coffee, tea, and pee breaks.

Gyms. I put this down near the bottom on the list, because gyms can be intimidating, especially if you're not in good shape or lack confidence. This probably isn't the best option for beginners, but keep in mind that women at gyms are hot. Yoga, tai chi, and other "mind/body" classes always attract fit, flexible, open-minded, and friendly women. Can you think of a better combination?

Personal Ads

To a lot of beginners, personal ads seem like the perfect compromise—or should I say crutch? After all, they take away the awkwardness of actually approaching and getting the attention of a beautiful woman, right? Well, that's exactly the problem. You're practicing to be a PUA here, and if you take a shortcut and go to the personals, you're never going to learn the skills you need to pick up women on your own. You'll always be a "paper guy," too scared to go out and hunt your prey, just waiting and hoping, instead, that they'll just fall into your lap.

This is no way to live. And besides, most of the women you'll meet through the personals are skanky.

College campuses. They can also be intimidating for the beginner (especially if you're over twenty-five), but this is where the college girls are. Enough said.

Nightclubs and Bars vs. the Real World

I am telling you that you don't want to go to a bar or nightclub to pick up women. But, you ask, aren't these places full of women? Is there really that much of a difference between a bar and a mall?

The answer to each of these questions is yes, but the second one is by far the more important. There really is a profound difference between approaching a woman in a nightclub and approaching her in a mall.

The difference: her expectations and her mind-set.

Remember, as an alpha male PUA you are always ready for a sexual encounter, no matter what the environment. But the woman is not. When you approach her in a mall, coffee shop, or

Hot Pants: A Street Pick-up Story

I used to work with a very beautiful woman who was a notorious ball-breaker. I saw her shoot down dozens of guys in bars without letting them get in a single word. In fact, I would say she was one of the hardest women to pick up I've ever known. In a bar situation, she was predisposed to laugh in poor chumps' faces, and she liked nothing better than to humiliate men for fun.

So I was surprised when she came into work one day excited about a man she had just met. Not only that, this guy had used a classic pick-up line!

The truth was, my female friend had a suit she thought made her look particularly hot (and she was right). Therefore, she was in the right mood—unsuspecting but feeling worthy of a compliment—when this normal-looking guy (but clearly a smooth operator schooled in the art of seduction) suddenly approached her on the street and complimented her on her suit. She was caught so unaware that she actually started talking to him instead of taking pleasure in torturing him . . . and, of course, he laid some moves on her and soon had her phone number.

The relationship only lasted a week, but from the stories I heard, it was a pretty passionate few days. The story got even better, at least in my mind, when I found out a while later that this woman—who had seemed so cold and ruthless—was pierced *down there* (if you know what I mean) and absolutely wild in the sack. Which is just to say that, if you take a woman when she's off her guard, you never know what wonderful surprises could be in store for you.

other non-traditional pick-up spots, you are more than likely going to take her by surprise. I've found that more often than not this works to your advantage. The woman wasn't expecting the compliment of your attention, so she's especially flattered that you noticed her. Because you've surprised her, she's much more likely to think your gesture was spontaneous and meant only for her. She is, therefore, much more likely not only to give you her number, but to remember you fondly when you call her later, even if you only had a brief conversation.

When you're working a bar or nightclub, on the other hand, the woman is expecting to be hit on. In fact, if she's a hot babe (and you'd never target a woman who wasn't, right?), then she's probably been hit on at least a couple of times already. Of course, this can work to your advantage because, thanks to this book, your approach will be much better than the sorry lines used by those other chumps. Also, she may very well be at the bar or club looking to get some action. That's what you're there for, after all, and women can play that game, too.

In general, though, I find it much easier to pleasantly surprise a woman than to try to impress her when she's on her guard. In a bar, the woman is psychologically prepared to blow you off. On the street, she's unsuspecting and more open to suggestion.

Casual Meetings

Girls want to meet their Prince Charming accidentally, as if by chance. They hate to admit to friends that they met you in a bar or nightclub, and meeting you on the street is only slightly better. They would much prefer to meet you at a private party (like a birthday or a wedding), through a mutual friend, or through an event organized around an interest or hobby. It's just more romantic that way, and women love romance.

Casual meetings are also much easier because, instead of being an unknown quantity, you come with the implicit recommendation of your friend or social group. You already have something in common, so you have something to talk about.

And if you've got a mutual friend, the women will naturally fling those doubts aside about you being a pervert, a loser, or (God forbid!) the kind of guy who picks up women all the time.

Of course, waiting to meet a woman in a casual situation really cuts down on your opportunities. That's why it's important to develop a few good pivots (see Chapter 6)—that is, women through whom you can meet other women. It's also a good idea to develop a few hobbies. Yes, picking up women and having hot sex is a great hobby, but it's always a good idea to be a bit more well-rounded.

However, hobbies and pivots do not equal permission to stop practicing your cold approach! Those street pick ups are the perfect way to hone your experience and confidence, because they are so difficult. Are you tired of me telling you that practice makes perfect? Are you thinking, "Enough already, I simply want to get laid tonight—I'll just take the easy prey"?

Well, let me tell you something, practice *does* make perfect. While you're still a beginner, you need to constantly be thinking about and working on your technique so that you won't just occasionally hit a few jackpots—you'll win at will and all the time. Once you graduate from drooling chump to experienced PUA, you'll enjoy the challenge and novelty of different environments . . . and, yes, I can assure you this is true, you'll actually get to the point where the hunt is as much fun as bedding down with the game.

So, no matter what your skill level, it's always best to shake things up. Casual meetings are easier, but pick-ups are more rewarding. The choice is yours, but a healthy mix of both is really the way to go. Besides, once your cold approach is seasoned, a casual meeting is like taking candy from a babe.

A Beginner's Course in Getting Comfortable with Women

Now that you've got the basic principles, it's time to actually make contact. I'll start at the beginning—and I mean the very beginning—and walk you all the way through the moment of actually making a move and picking up the girl. Believe me, if you've never spoken to a strange woman before, the first move is not to go out and try to pick up a hot babe. And no, we're not going to practice on the ugly ones either.

Instead, I'm going to walk you through a series of steps that will teach you how to talk to women in non-sexual situations. That way, the pressure's off, as is the fear of rejection. I'm not going to set a time frame for you to go through these steps. Move at your own pace, but always push yourself to the next level. If you're experienced (or confident) enough to skip these basics, then go forward to the next section.

The faster you get through these beginner stages, after all, the sooner you'll be bedding down.

Step 1: Eye Contact

In order to seduce a woman, you have to get her to notice you. That's rule number one. Rule number two is that you want her to notice you *in a positive manner*. When you look a woman in the eyes, you get her attention—and you project an image of power. You're not intimidated; you know what you want. That turns a woman on.

The goal is not to stare, but to lock eyes with a woman. Staring is creepy; locking eyes is powerful. Here's what you do:

Go down to the mall and walk around. When you see a beautiful woman walking toward you, wait until she is about thirty feet away and then start glancing at her eyes. When she glances at you, lock onto her eyes and try to hold the contact. Do not look from eye to eye, blink, or glance away. Stay focused on one eye, and hold that contact as long as you can without turning your head.

One of three things will happen. About half the time the woman won't notice you. Don't force it (that's staring and it's creepy), just keep walking and look for the next girl. About a third of the time, she will lock eyes with you for an instant and then look away. If that happens, you should look away too and just keep walking.

In a few cases, though, the woman will actually lock onto your eyes and hold the contact. If this happens, do not react. Just continue walking without changing your facial expression or altering your pace. Only break the contact when she breaks the contact. Sometimes she will smile. If she does, smile back.

If you're just starting out, don't force yourself to smile first. Keep in mind though, that according to statistics, smiles are mirrored back in 85 percent of all cases. So if you're feeling playful and have had enough of simple eye contact, you can advance to the next level. Smile first and see for yourself whether the statistics are true. Besides, it can be great fun making a girl smile just by walking by.

Don't forget though that this only applies to situations where you have already locked eyes with the woman and she is not looking away. For whatever reason, she is intrigued by you and has allowed herself to be locked into eye contact with you. This is a very positive sign, so don't take it for granted! You've established a "direct connection" to her brain and emotions, so this is the perfect opportunity to make that emotion a positive one for her—all within a couple of seconds.

Eventually, if you see the same woman on a regular basis, she may become responsive enough to say "hi" when you pass each other. Say "hi" back, but keep on walking. Don't worry about "what next?" You're only practicing eye contact right now, so the pressure is off. After all, you haven't made a move, and neither has she, but you've learned to make a connection.

Step 2: The Good Samaritan

Eye contact is one thing, conversation is another. If you're intimidated by talking to beautiful women, try something totally innocent. When you see a beautiful woman, walk up to her and helpfully point out that her heel looks loose or that her shoe is untied or that she has a little mascara on her face . . . and then walk away.

Hopefully, during the two seconds it took to walk up to her, you've had time to actually spot something that needs adjusting or correcting, in which case you can indeed be the Good Samaritan. If, however, everything about her looks perfect, just "point out" something anyway—tell her she has a speck of dirt on her face—even if it is not true. Her self-image won't be shattered, because you're being a gentleman.

Meanwhile, you're learning not to be fazed by the beauty of even the most beautiful women. And they will respect you because, unlike those AFCs, you weren't drooling over their perfect looks. Instead, you were helping them with something that is extremely important to them—their appearance. And then, instead of trying to use that opportunity to get in their pants, you just walked away. What a guy!

Even better, you've gained the experience of not being supplicative to beautiful women, not addressing them from below, but from above—by teasing them a bit and then leaving them puzzled about you and your intentions. In other words, you're acting like an alpha male, which, at least in the minds of these particular women, makes you an alpha male. Do this enough times, and you'll be well on your way to obtaining and keeping the successful PUA attitudes that will get you exactly the kind of women you've always dreamed about.

Just remember the Three Second Rule when being a Good Samaritan—no stalling—and you'll be amazed how much this simple trick will help your confidence and technique.

Step 3: The Compliment

The Compliment is the same as the Good Samaritan, except this time you're actually conversing with (as opposed to just saying a few words to) the woman. Instead of making up an excuse to say one thing to her, you're actually going to segue into a topic. This will not only get you talking, but it will help you become more attentive because, as always, you only have three seconds to come up with a compliment that isn't generic, but actually makes sense for this particular woman.

Remember, you're still under no pressure to pick this woman up. Although giving a compliment is more difficult than the Good Samaritan technique—you have no ready excuse for approaching her and you're putting yourself at risk by expressing something positive about the woman—you're just practicing talking to women. However, as you progress to this stage you should set yourself the goal of following up your initial compliment with *at least two questions*. In other words, you're about to engage in an actual conversation.

The key is to ask the right questions. Never ask a question with a yes or no answer. Always ask an open-ended question that will lead to further discussion. For instance, if your opener is to compliment her dress, ask her where she got it or what it's made of. The more you know on the subject the better, but don't get bogged down in trying to be too smart or clever. It's still just conversation.

And don't worry, further along in this book you'll find more in-depth information about what kind of compliments to pay and what kind to avoid.

Step 4: Avoid Becoming the Friend

Good eye contact, being the Good Samaritan, paying the right kind of compliment, and having a casual short conversation thanks to a few open-ended questions are all well and good. But, even after such a promising start, a lot of guys let their encounters degenerate into . . . the dreaded Friend Zone. Being labeled a friend in the woman's mind is the kiss of death. Who needs another friend? There are ways to "rise from the dead" after having become a friend, but you're better off avoiding it at the start.

Avoiding the Friend Zone is really all about attitude—but since you're still a beginner, you probably don't yet have the ability to give off a casual, sexual vibe. Therefore, you need to up the ante as simply and directly as possible.

Once you've mastered Step 3, and you're feeling comfortable in casual conversations with beautiful women, it's time to take control of those conversations. Of course, you won't be making a rude remark or asking an obnoxious question; that would end the conversation. Instead, ask the seemingly simple yet covertly tricky question, "Are you the kind of person I should get to know?" You can even ask that out of the blue— since this is your first conversation anyway, the question is relevant no matter what you've talked about so far.

The trick here is to catch the woman off guard and remind her that, however innocent-sounding your conversation might have been so far, there is a purpose to it all. You've reminded her that it is not just some idle chit-chat, it is about a man and a woman getting to know each other. You've given her some food for thought—sexual thought.

Even better, now the tables are turned and she is the one being evaluated, not you. Since she's probably not used to something like this, she'll probably make an effort not to lose face in front of you. In the unlikely case she blurts out "no," she'll only be putting herself down. With any other answer, though, the obvious next question is, "Why?" Now you're having the kind of conversation PUAs have!

Your Home Is Your Love-Nest

Women hate dirty, lazy, thoughtless men. So why are you letting your house or apartment send that message about you? This is the place where you are going to bring women to have sex, so you'd better make sure your pad is prepared for love and projects the right image from the moment the woman walks in. Otherwise, she's going to turn tail and run . . . and not to your bedroom. Here are a few tips:

- Keep your place neat. Make especially sure that the floors are clean, your clothes are in your drawers, and there is definitely no visible garbage.
- Keep the temperature warm enough so that both of you can get comfortably naked, but not so warm you're going to break out in a sweat.

A Game of Crash and Burn

Here's a suggestion from PUA Razor Cat that I recommend to anyone having trouble overcoming that crippling fear of rejection. For you beginners, it might be easier to travel to a different side of town or a location you rarely visit to play this game. Razor Cat calls it "Crash and Burn," and its object is to make you comfortable with rejection.

What you need to do is make a fool of yourself trying to pick up women. Give them the worst lines, double entendres, and gimmicks you can think of. This is the time to pull out those vintage seventies era pick-up lines. This may be the only time when a PUA will say, "If I said you had a beautiful body, would you hold it against me?" without shame. Your goal is to crash and burn. Repeatedly. See how ridiculous you can make yourself to the woman. You'll find that you can actually have fun getting shot down if you make it your goal. Once you discover that crashing and burning isn't really that bad, you'll grow desensitized to the fear of rejection.

What you'll learn is that failure isn't looking like an idiot with a woman. Failure is not trying. Losing one woman isn't the end of the world—it's just losing with *one* woman out of the millions of Honey Bunnies out there.

Failure is just your next step on the road to success.

- Lights on a dimmer are always a good idea. Barring that, have some candles handy. Actually, always make sure you have a healthy store of candles—they are a huge turn-on for women.
- Always have some chocolate on hand, and some white wine or champagne cooling in the fridge. Any sweet is good, but chocolate in particular is a major aphrodisiac.

Although I don't personally recommend using alcohol, neither to boost your own confidence nor to soften up a lady, alcohol in moderation is classy and romantic. Never intentionally try to get a woman drunk—that tactic is for rapists, not pick-up artists!

- Make sure the place smells nice. Scented candles are perfect for this, since they'll also help set the mood.

- Have appropriate music. Not Barry White or anything too overtly get-it-on, but Enya, movie soundtracks, and other female-friendly choices. Classical music is perfect, and these CDs are so cheap at most record stores that you can buy a duplicate to give her as a reminder of your wonderful evening.

- Protective measures: have them handy but out of sight, and know where they are. Keep a few in several different rooms—you never know where the evening is headed.

- The bathroom . . . it's clean, right? A dirty bathroom is a huge turnoff, so make sure it is the absolutely nicest cleanest place in your apartment or house. The only thing in plain sight should be quality brands of cologne, shampoo, and other toiletries that show your attention to detail.

- Always have available big fluffy terry-towels, two robes, and an extra toothbrush still in the pack. Having more pillows than your average home is a good idea, too.

- Remember to unplug the phone *before* the action gets heavy.

Just Say, "Hi"

For some of us, the best woman is that stranger we see every morning at the coffee shop, or that woman we often pass on the sidewalk after work. If you're a dreamer, that's probably the girl for you—and the reason you picked up this book. I've already told you to ditch that dream and start having sex with other women—women you aren't so emotionally attached to— right now.

But here, right before we enter the pick-up zone, I'll give you the simple approach of your dreams. It's perfect for a beginner because you don't even have to make a real move or show your alpha male side in any way. All it takes is a lot of consistency and persistence (which is why it's strictly beginners or fun-on-the-side only), but getting your foot in the door before making your real move can be to your advantage. While you're using this approach on your dream girl, you'll also be out there trying the more direct approach on dozens of beautiful women. And you'll be learning how to satisfy them like only an experienced mover can.

So here's what you do. When you see the girl you like but can't approach, just make eye contact and say, "Hi." Then smile, turn away, and continue what you were doing. When you see her the next time (Oh, joy!), do the same thing. Continue to do this for as long as you keep seeing her. I guarantee that by the third "hi," she'll start wondering about you. By the fifth "hi," she'll be wondering why you never talk to her. By the tenth "hi," she'll be wondering why you don't approach her. At the twentieth "hi," she'll get so intrigued she'll actually start talking to you. She'll probably ask you about yourself, and she may even ask you directly why you never go any further than "hi." Is there something wrong with her? Do you know her from somewhere? Keep your answers vague and mysterious—after all, you've had twenty "encounters" already, so she's going to feel like she knows you, even though you've only exchanged one word. You're going to have to do some work from here (and you'll learn how later in this book), but guess what? You're talking with the gorgeous woman of your dreams, she's intrigued by you, and it required almost no effort or chance of embarrassment.

There are, of course, some downsides to this approach. You may stop bumping into her for some reason, which can be particularly devastating if she had actually started to show interest

---

What Am I Trying to Do Here Anyway?

No, the answer isn't get laid. That's far too simple, and totally unhelpful. The key to seduction is to *make the woman want sex, and to want to have it with you.* Your desires should never come into play: they are a given. Your goal is to work on her desires, to drive her almost to the point of ecstasy, and to make her think about how wonderful sex with you would be. Once she's there, the rest is just a matter of steering her in the right direction.

---

in you. Or, if you don't see her often enough (at least twice a week), there's a good chance your smiling and making eye contact won't be consistent enough to build intrigue. And lastly, of course, this plan takes a monstrous amount of time to develop, and as a PUA you should hate to measure a conquest in months rather than minutes.

Still, for a beginner, a love-sick AFC, or an alpha male interested in playing out a long-range seduction just for kicks, the "hi" approach can't be beat.

PART

The Pick-up

CHAPTER 3

The Approach

The Importance of a First Impression

In general, a woman makes a decision about whether or not she will sleep with a man very early in a first encounter. This doesn't mean that if she likes your moves, she's *going* to sleep with you. You still have to follow through and take her from initial interest to wet-panties desire.

It does mean, however, that she can rule you out based on a first impression. And no, I didn't say based on looks. Get over it already! Women are interested in the way you present yourself, which is why acting like a desperate and horny—or simply nice and wimpy—AFC produces nothing for you. Ever. If a woman has decided in the first thirty seconds that she is not interested in sleeping with you, no amount of pursuit or persuasion will change her mind—unless you learn to change yourself first. Many men have wasted their precious time and energy by ignoring (or not knowing) that they have fallen into the dreaded LJBF (Let's Just Be Friends) zone. If a woman likes you, it's just a matter of convincing her you're a boyfriend not a friend. If she doesn't like you, her mind is made up—she won't be your lover or girlfriend or wife or anything at all.

If you've already fallen into the LJBF zone with a woman (because you had not yet picked up this book), don't despair. You can still change her mind, since the techniques in this book will teach you how. If you can leave your old AFC habits behind and act like a man, she will forget all about the old you . . . in time. It will take considerably more time than if you had made the right impression on her in the first place, but if you're a PUA it can be done. Now that you're different and can make her feel different, present yourself to her anew and watch the fireworks ignite.

This, of course, does nothing to lessen the importance of a first impression. So, instead of trying to undo the damage of past bad impressions, let's get started looking at how to make the right first impression. This is called The Approach.

3S: Practical Applications

You're worshipping the Three Second Rule, right? As soon as you enter a room you're moving on a woman, right? Or are you hesitating . . . wondering . . . stalling . . .

The Three Second Rule is easily abused by those who lack the confidence to use it properly. They start thinking: What does it meant to spot a girl? Does it mean eye contact? If so, did we really make eye contact, or should I wait for confirmation from a second look? Now it looks like she's talking to someone else, maybe I'll just wait . . .

Stop already. Can't you see what you're doing? You're over-thinking the situation, the very thing 3S is supposed to prevent. Let's just step back for a minute and understand what 3S is all about: getting you off the sidelines and into the action *immediately*.

I do mean immediately, because the three seconds begin as soon as you notice each other. This doesn't mean eye contact. Even the most casual glance starts the clock. If she even glances for a second at your side of the room, you had better make your move. Don't stop to wonder if she's seen you or not. That's hesitating, and hesitating is for guys who go home alone.

The Party Exception

Always worship the Three Second Rule, no exceptions. Still, I'm going to give you one exception, and that's if you go to a party. You're going to be there for a while, the atmosphere is low-key, the drinks are free, so it's acceptable in this case to just lay back and watch the social scene develop. You'll soon notice that some girls seem lost, and that some of these "lost girls" are hot as hell. These girls will be extremely easy to talk to because they'll latch on to anything to stop the loneliness. Go ahead and cut them some slack if the conversation starts off a little awkward; she obviously doesn't know anyone at this party, and that's a hard situation for anyone to be in. She's lucky you found her!

The easiest time to apply 3S is when you are new to a situation. When you open a door or round a corner, people notice you because you are a change in a static environment. So every time you get ready to enter a room—whether it's a bar, a coffee shop, or a friend's party—you need to be ready to worship 3S. Every time you round a corner, you should be prepared to approach that beautiful woman that's sure to be headed your way. Just shut your brain off and go on *instinct*.

There is, of course, an exception to the 3S Rule. This occurs when you spot a pretty girl, but you are clearly tied up in a conversation with someone else. In this case, the three seconds will start counting from the moment you are free to approach. The timing doesn't matter as much as the fact that you make it obvious that you're leaving that conversation—implying that you're leaving it for her—instead of having the other person leave you first.

The same is true on her end. She's noticed you, but she's stuck talking with a friend. No problem, just wait until he walks away (he always will eventually), and approach her immediately. Or, alternatively, inject yourself into a group conversation using the Group Tactics described in Chapter 6.

But what if you hesitate? Is all lost? Yes—and no. If you botch 3S, the best idea is to scratch that girl off your list. But don't worry, there are plenty of gorgeous, fun-loving women in the world. Just don't make the same mistake twice.

General Guidelines on Approaching

The most important aspect of your approach is that, within thirty seconds, you must make the girl find you entertaining and intriguing. If she thinks other guys are more entertaining and interesting than you, she will always excuse herself (sometimes politely, sometimes not so politely) in the hopes that one of those other studs will approach her.

The key is to remain mysterious. Never give too much away about yourself in the approach. You don't want to tell her something that will turn her off in your opening (you don't know her yet, so how do you know she doesn't hate your profession or your alma mater or your politics?) and, besides, the first part of any seduction encounter is all about her. And for God's sake, never be negative. Always be positive in your opening—don't complain— not about the atmosphere at the party, the taste of your coffee, and especially not about your life. That's a real downer, and it only serves to get her thinking about all the negatives of being with you, when she should be thinking about the positives.

Instead of bringing her down, try bringing her up with a little humor. Women love a guy who makes them laugh because it lifts their mood and makes them forget their troubles. They can't be depressed if they're laughing, and even better, they've just lowered their protective shield and let you into their personal space. Or, as Ross Jeffries (www.seduction.com) puts it:

1. Laughter puts a woman at ease and off her guard.
2. Getting her laughing shows that you are confident and don't take your meeting too seriously, unlike a desperate

hard-up loser who *has to* succeed. You are a fun guy, enjoying your exciting life, and creating an opportunity for her to step into it . . . if she plays her cards right.

3. Humor is a test to see if she has a personality. If she's mean and unhappy, why bother?

Don't get me wrong. Humor is tricky; it simply isn't easy to make a stranger laugh. That's why some PUAs swear off the humorous approach entirely. But remember: if you can make a woman you just met laugh, you are almost assured of closing the encounter with her number, if not a kiss.

The key is, as always, to act quickly. If your approach bombs (no smile) you need to be ready to follow up with another conversation starter (and if that bombs, you probably have one more chance before you eject that humorless hag). If she laughs, you need to be ready to keep the conversation flowing toward a pattern, eliciting values, or any other technique described in the Initiating a Conversation portion of this guide (see p. 62).

Remember these general guidelines to the approach when reading the other portions to this section, such as Fun and Games (p. 73), and even Your Last Chance (p. 76)—mystery, positiveness, and humor are important no matter where you are in your approach or which technique you try.

The First Words out of Your Mouth

You've used 3S and you're approaching a woman. She's noticed you coming, and you can tell she's waiting for you to say something. Maybe she looks nervous; maybe she looks ready to blow you off; maybe she looks excited. It doesn't matter. That's all in your mind—her mind hasn't been revealed yet. You've already set your attitude to a positive, "this woman needs me" approach. Now your seduction techniques are going to influence her feelings about you.

What do you say? The first words out of your mouth can make or break the conversation, so you'd better make them good. There are a number of different techniques you can employ, such as neghits and GM style, which we'll discuss later, but you're best off with the most straight-forward approach possible: commenting on the environment.

The Chump

It's a little hot in the bar, so you go up to the woman and say: "So, it's kind of hot in here." Bad idea. For one thing, that is a lame and pointless statement that simply shows you have nothing interesting to say. Even worse, it sounds like a pick-up line. It calls for a simple yes or no answer, a major mistake unless you're anticipating that answer and already have an open-ended follow-up question in mind. Lastly, you're focusing on a negative, making her think about something uncomfortable instead of something pleasant. You seem like a whiner, a major turnoff for women.

The PUA

With experience, you'll realize that a line like that needs to trade on the sexuality of the word "hot." For instance, you could say, "I was just thinking how hot it is in here, and one possible answer I came up with is that it might be because of you. So what's your story?"

That's a classic opener, followed immediately by an open-ended question. Why does that work, when the first example doesn't? Here's what you need to keep in mind:

1. By commenting on the environment in a neutral manner you're doing what is called "pacing her reality." This means that you're saying out loud what she is probably thinking, thus forcing her to agree with you and creating positive common ground.

2. You're *sort* of paying her a compliment, because you're also leaving a door open to the possibility that it is *not* hot there because of her. The point here is to get her wonder-

ing whether you were actually paying her a compliment or not. Being able to create a state of intrigue and confusion in a woman's mind is one of the main things that differentiates the PUAs from the ordinary chumps. Most women have the chumps figured out a mile away; the PUAs keep them surprised and guessing, forcing them to follow along. And once her mind is yours, the rest will soon follow.

3. Now that you've derailed her train of thought, turn the focus to her. The age-old "So, what's a girl like you doing in a place like this?" question can all too often end with, "I'm waiting for my boyfriend." Whoops. On the other hand, "What's your story?" is a perfect open-ended question, because it allows her to talk about absolutely anything that pops to her mind. Try it a few times, and you'll be surprised how many completely different types of answers you get.

4. While she's talking, you're listening intently and starting to piece together a picture of her, her likes and dislikes, interests, and if you get lucky, even some hints of her dreams and fantasies, all of which you can use later to fulfill her and become the man of her dreams. Ultimately, your goal here is to have her block out everything in her world except you—and the wonderful time she is having with you.

In conclusion: Don't stop talking until you've given her a question she has to answer. Don't talk more than ten to fifteen seconds before giving her the opening. Always remember that the goal of the approach is to get you into conversation as quickly as possible. It's not the amount of time spent in the opening gambit; it's the quality. The next section outlines a few simple approaches, all of which should satisfy the requirements just outlined. The approach isn't going to score the goal. It's just the setup. So, get through it as quickly as possible and move on to the Initiating a Conversation portion.

Simple Approaches

Here are a few simple approaches that have worked for many poor chumps over the years. You can either add these to your own bag of tricks, or, even better, you can use them to create your own personal style. Is it okay to use standard openers on a lot of different women? Of course. Just be flexible enough to adapt them to each situation, and make sure they don't sound like a canned speech you give all the girls.

Always remember, though, both here and throughout the book, that the examples given are not mantras, magic combinations of words, the uttering of which will make all women fall into your arms. They are just examples.

Your job is not to memorize them word for word, then deliver them later to a mystified woman like a bad actor at summer stock. You won't believe how many men make this simple mistake, with the end result being that their approaches are spectacular disasters.

Your job is to study these examples in order to understand their underlying dynamics. You need to understand what mental images are being used, what kind of feelings they provoke in a woman, and what they make a woman feel and imagine.

Sure, you can start off by memorizing the examples that are the most to your liking. But those are not the ones that are going to work in real life. The ones that are going to work are those that you make up yourself, on the fly, by applying the *principles* that are used in these examples.

The Subtle Approach

Example 1 (best if you don't have to approach from too far away): "I was just thinking of experiences, how sometimes the most commonplace thing can be incredibly wonderful and absorbing, like when you were a kid and you went to a museum and just got lost in the delight of what you were seeing. I'm sure you know what I'm talking about, because you've probably had an experience like that before. (She's involuntarily nodding). What's one of your most interesting experiences?"

Example 2 Start by thanking the woman. She may or may not ask you why you're thanking her, but it doesn't matter—launch into the next part of the opener. Tell her that you were feeling down, not having the best day ever, though you couldn't really pin down anything horrible either. Then the sight of her lit up your day and made you feel a bit better. Her smile just made you want to smile too. Then say that you know she didn't come out just to make you feel better, and ask her what is going on in her life.

How Was Your Day?

There's nothing more classic than walking up to a woman and asking about her day. This works best in a social situation, like a party or some sort of gathering, but it's equally good in any non-pick-up (in other words, non-bar) environment. And, of course, don't use this opener first thing in the morning. Waiting at least until afternoon is always advised.

You: So, how was your day?
Her: Great!

Perfect. She's in a good mood, and since you're in a good mood she's going to feel some instant rapport with you. You smile and say, "So was mine. What did you do?"

But what if she says . . .

Her: Awful.

No problem. If her day was bad, she's going to want to talk about it, and that gives you the perfect opportunity to show that you're an empathetic, understanding guy that can make her feel wonderful, even on the worst of days. You put your hand on her shoulder and say, "I'm sorry. What happened?"

But what if she says:

Her: Okay, I guess.

This is a tough one, but not too tough. Clearly, she's either trying to brush you off or there's nothing in her day she wants to talk about. So you say, "Well then, what about yesterday?"

Her: It was fine.

Medic! We need fifty ccs of adrenaline over here STAT. This girl is about to fall into a coma. It's time for you to start creating some fun. If you can lift this girl out of the doldrums, she'll definitely be yours.

You (*raising your hands like you're measuring about a foot in length*): So, you don't feel this excited? [She smirks, so you narrow your hands.] How about this excited? [Was that a slight muscle twitch you just saw? Is she starting to come around? You hold up one hand, thumb and finger an inch apart.] Could you possibly, at the very least, be entertaining the thought of being this excited about life? [She smiles . . . and if you can bring a smile to the catatonic, she'll love you for it. If she doesn't smile, just walk away. That joyless hag isn't worth your time.]

You Look Exactly Like . . .

Here's a brilliant twist on an old classic by Clifford, of *Clifford's Seduction Newsletter*: Clifford suggests walking up to a woman and telling her that that she "looks like . . ." and then pausing. He drags it out, looking at her carefully, and keeps saying that she "looks like . . ." without telling her who or what. The woman will pay attention, wondering what comparison he's about to make. Once he sees that she's interested, he judges her personality. He usually ends by saying, "You look exactly like . . . someone I should get to know better" or, ". . . somebody I'd like to meet." If he senses that she's uncomfortable or doesn't have a sense of humor, he backs off and says that on second thought, she doesn't look like the person he was thinking of, but he'd like to get to know her better anyway.

Remember to close this opener out, as with all openers, with an open-ended question, such as, "So, what brings you out here today?" And, yes, you should always avoid that old standby of the chump set, "Do you come here often?" unless . . .

The Familiar Approach

One of the easiest and most effective ways to get a stranger to talk to you is to act like you know her. Just start in the middle, as if you're picking up a conversation with an old acquaintance. Skip all the opening lines (they suck and girls hate them) and introductions (she's going to offer her name and phone number soon anyway). It's important not to convey the image that you are hitting on her, so be friendly (not fawning and drooling), confident (not trembling and stuttering), and humorous.

Many times, the woman will play along like she knows you . . . until it's too late. Other times, she'll ask straight out how you know her. Know that this moment is going to occur at some point, and have an answer in mind. You can either take the honest approach and tell her that you didn't know her before, but you do now . . . and you definitely want to get to know her better. Or you could take the "mistaken identity" approach, modified from Clifford's advice above.

Modification 1: Fool her into thinking she knows you. Kevin Kupal, mindlist subscriber, advocates this modification of the familiar approach, which uses suggestion to convince the woman that she knows you. He glances at a woman, then looks back as if he's surprised to see her. At this point, the woman may begin talking with him. If not, he opens by saying that the woman looks familiar, that they must know each other from somewhere else. He asks her if he looks familiar to her too. If the woman says that she might recognize him from somewhere, he invites her to share a coffee with him to figure out where they've met.

Modification 2: The high five

> I give girls high fives all the time . . . the next time I see them
> I say, "I remember you!" and then we're instant friends! I
> will also go up to a girl and put my hand up in a high-five
> position, then when they slap it I'll just start talking.
>
> —Craig

Crazy, yes, but I've used it myself—and it works.

The Stunning Approach

I picked this one up from the master of seduction Ross Jeffries (www.seduction.com), and it has become one of my personal favorites. However, I hesitate to put it here because it's a
pretty advanced technique. In general, telling a woman she looks
stunning as an opener is the wrong approach, because it makes
it seem like you're being a supplicating, overly horny AFC who's
only after her body. That's why, for this approach, it's all in the
delivery. You have to talk slowly, radiating genuineness, confidence, and relaxed power. The key is to be low-key. If you come
off horny or needy, this approach will never work.

The opener involves walking directly up to a woman, exud-
ing power but not rushing, and saying, "Excuse me (although
you're really not excusing yourself for making her feel really,
really good in just a few seconds), I just wanted to tell you . . .
(pause to create anticipation) I think you're absolutely stunning . . . and I really wanted to meet you."

You've knocked her back on her heels, and she's going to need
a moment to respond. Don't let her catch her breath. Immediately
step forward *slightly* into her personal space and shake her hand.
Now, and this is key, don't let go! Keep holding on as you continue to talk to her and look her directly in the eyes. A majority of
women—maybe 60 percent—will pull away and stomp off like
you're a creep. With the rest, you've made an extremely personal
and sexually charged impression . . . in about five seconds. This
approach is high risk, and there's a definitely chance you could
look like a horny loser, but there's also high reward.

Do not use this approach on women who are truly stunning. They've heard it all before, so it's just going to sound like another pathetic come-on to them. The power of the stunning approach is actually in stunning the woman, or in other words, pleasantly surprising her. If she doesn't feel stunning, or doesn't hear that kind of compliment often, you have a much better chance of success. Do not, of course, use this opener on truly unattractive women. Why? Because you should never pick up ugly women! Have enough confidence to aim high.

The Dramatic Approach

The goal of the dramatic approach is to make a scene—and I mean the kind of scene that will attract the attention of everyone within a mile, including the woman—and then reveal to her that the only reason you did that extraordinary bizarre or embarrassing thing was to get her attention. Being willing to embarrass yourself just to meet her is a real sign of commitment, and it makes her feel pretty darn special. It also implies that you're spontaneous and crazy (in a good way), but also courageous and strong-willed; in other words, exactly the kind of man many girls have wet dreams about. Here's an example of the dramatic approach, developed out of a pickup in an ebook called *Sweep Women Off Their Feet and Into Your Bed*, which can be found on the Internet. For safety reasons, I can't recommend this specific incident, but you'll get the idea.

> The author was driving down the street, and he saw a beautiful woman standing on the sidewalk. Inconveniencing the other cars on the road, he slammed on his brakes, put on his hazard lights, and ran out of the car. Needless to say, he got the woman's attention. When she realized that he was running to her, she was even more surprised. He told her that she was the kind of woman that literally stopped traffic. He said that he wasn't the kind of person that usually did this sort of thing, but that he had to get to know her. She was so surprised and flattered that she gave him her name. After parking the car a little more safely, the two went out together for coffee.

The Cellular Approach

Technology is a fantastic tool, so why not use it? Let's say you're sitting in a public place, and you see a hot babe sitting nearby, close enough that she can hear whatever you say. Your best option is to make eye contact, smile, and use the Three Second Rule. If you're too much of an AFC for the direct approach (and you better get over it pretty quickly), and you have a cell phone on you, try this little cheat.

If you have a ringer tester or volume control, use it to pretend that the phone is ringing. If not, just act like you're on vibrate and that someone just vibed you. Pick up the phone and start talking *about her*. Start by implying that your friend called about a woman and that you're no longer with her, then mention that there's a beautiful woman here right now, that she keeps looking your way but she's shy, that you admire her self-control, but she's sending mixed signals. At this point, she should be giving you a clear sign of her intentions by either ignoring you or giving you a shy smile. Take the hint and run with it—either away from her or toward her, whichever she wants.

This is a very passive and slightly wussy strategy, but it can be a nice change of pace and a whole lot of fun. Just remember to turn your ringer off before talking to your fake friend, as a real call at the wrong time can be pretty embarrassing.

The Pez Approach

Here's a classic that's sure to get a laugh. And it's almost foolproof. All you do is walk up to a woman, tilt your head to the side and look serious, and wait for her to give you that "what do you want, creep?" look. Crack a smile and pull out your Pez dispenser.

You: Pez?

Her *(laughing)*: Sure. I love Pez.

You: Didn't your mom warn you about taking candy from strangers?

Her: Yeah . . .

You: Isn't it funny how forbidden things can be so exciting?

The Collision Approach

I usually don't advocate using a line, but here's an exception to the rule because it's so darn effective, fun, and harmless (even the blow off here is totally painless). The "collision" begins when you see a beautiful woman walking down the street toward you. You work it out so that you accidentally get in front of her and cut her off. "Excuse me," she says, to which you reply, "No problem. You would have stopped me in my tracks even if we hadn't bumped into each other."

One of two things will happen. She will move on without comment, which just goes to show (and painlessly, too) that she's not the kind of fun-loving girl you want to spend time with. The other reaction is for her to laugh. If she does, hit her with this classic from Ross Jeffries (www.seduction.com): "I'm glad you laughed, because you really are breathtaking, and I wanted to get a glimpse of the personality inside the beauty. It's great to meet a woman with more going on than just her looks."

Did you catch that line? Good, because it's important. That line has scored more action than just about any other line I've ever learned. It is the perfect response to a laugh *in any approach situation*. Once you've laid that line on a woman, you can jump to just about any subject you want and, almost without fail, start engaging her in a wonderful conversation.

The Pick-up Line

Pick-up lines are lame. Their lack of originality and supplicative, horny-but-clueless AFC quality will backfire almost every time . . . *if* you use them seriously. Pick-up lines should only be used as a last resort if you've applied the Three Second Rule, yet are totally choking and can't think of anything to say. In that case, you've got to throw one out there, but you better make sure it's a curveball by introducing it like this:

You approach, smile, and drop a pick-up line on her. She gives you a blank look, but before her jaw can drop you say, "I'm just kidding. My friend was telling me about some lines he's heard some guys use, and I always wanted to see what the reaction would be. What do you think about this one?" Second pick-up line. If she responds—doesn't matter if it's good or bad, as long as she's not ignoring you—keep going. Eventually, one of your lines should get a laugh, the holy grail of success. At that point, turn the conversation to her by asking if she's heard any good ones lately. Now you're halfway to a conversation.

So, without further ado, here's a list of assorted pick-up lines. Remember, these are only to be used as a last-ditch resource in case of a choke, or incorporated into an opening gambit that plays on the fact that all pick-up lines suck. And, yes, I warned you, these are cheesy:

- (Delivered rapid-fire.) "Hi! Do you have a boyfriend? Would you like a better one? Answer the second question first."
- If she's alone, point to a nearby guy and say, "Is that your boyfriend? Good, because you can do a lot better than that."
- "Excuse me. I just wanted to tell you that if God made anything nicer than your smile, he's keeping it to himself."
- "Let's go to my place and do all the things I'll tell everyone we did anyway."
- "If I said you had a beautiful body would you hold it against me?"
- "Is it hot in here, or is it just you?"

- "Do you believe in love at first sight, or do I have to walk past again?"
- "Pardon me. I seem to have lost my phone number. Can I borrow yours?"
- *This one might confuse her—it's supposed to*: "If I were to ask you for sex, would the answer be the same as the answer to this question?"
- "Excuse me, I just noticed you noticing me and I just wanted to give you notice that I noticed you, too."
- As you walk by, turn and say, "Excuse me, did you touch my ass? No? I guess it was just wishful thinking."
- *To a woman in a tight outfit*: "That's a great outfit you're almost wearing."
- *If she was checking you out*: "Shall we talk or continue to flirt from a distance?"
- "Are you as good as they say you are?"
- *If she's not that attractive*: "What does it feel like to be the most beautiful woman in the room?"
- *Again, if she's just average looking but the best option around*: "You know, you might be asked to leave soon. You're making all the other women look bad."
- "Your place or mine? Tell you what, I'll flip a coin. Head at my place, tail at yours."
- "What's a nice girl like you doing in a place like this?"
- "Hi. Do you know any good opening lines?"

Now, a lot of these lines are funny (kind of), and women love to laugh, so they can definitely be used to your advantage. In fact, while these lines always suck as openers, they can sometimes be the first transition from a pleasant, happy, intriguing, sexy conversation to propositioning her. For instance, the coin flip line above is a terrible opener (if used seriously), but it can be a very effective way to invite her over because, after a stimu-

---

Classic Comebacks

For your amusement, here are a few classic female rebuttals you might hear if you make the mistake of using a pick-up line AFC-style.

Him: I'd like to call you some time. What's your number?

Her: It's in the phone book.

Him: But I don't know your name.

Her: It's in the phone book too.

Him: What do you say to a little fuck?

Her: Go away, little fuck.

Her *(after hearing a pick-up line)*: I like your approach. Now let's see your departure.

---

lating conversation, it's playful, fun, and totally appropriate. So sneer all you want, but you may just find yourself using these stupid lines—and getting great results with them.

Gimmicks

"Are you into metaphysics? Do you believe in astrology? Astral projection? ESP? Tarot cards? What's that you say? You think it's a bunch of crap? Well, so do I. But guess what? Women eat this stuff like candy, so I pretend to be interested in all of it!"

—Ross Jeffries (www.seduction.com)

Gimmicks are nothing to be ashamed of. They're far cooler and more interesting than pick-up lines, and they can be a lot of fun for both you and the woman. Ross Jeffries's favorite gimmick is handwriting analysis. All you need is a Grapho-Deck (which you can find at www.myhandwriting.com), and you'll know every-

---

A Few Palm-Reading Tips

- The dominant hand is usually the one read, so ask her if she's right or left-handed. It's even better to hold both her hands, though, so read her dominant hand to her, then grab her other hand and use it to "show" her her inner potential. (Yes, this is actually palmistry—and a perfect chance to put her "potential" to work for you.)

- If she has two fate lines (running vertically in center of palm), and the break happens at a younger age (further up toward the fingers), that means something traumatic happened in her life. Explain this to her, then ask her what it was. This creates instant rapport.

- If her fate line is broken in her future (the line runs bottom to top in relation to age), then you've got the perfect chance to predict her future. Be serious about this, and try to play along with her desires—whether it's to get a new job, to travel, or maybe even to move to a new city. You're learning valuable information here.

- Always predict something positive, but don't forget to show her how you came to that conclusion (even if it's total bullshit).

- When you're done with the reading, hold her hand, look her in the eye, then kiss her lightly on the fingertips.

---

thing you need to be a master of this pick-up in about, well, five minutes.

However, I prefer something a little more hands on, literally—palm reading. The best part of palm reading is that it gets you instant kino because you're going to be holding and rubbing her hand. Then, once you start "reading" her palm, you can launch into all kinds of suggestive stuff, like the fact that it looks like she's highly sexed, physically responsive, and other similar titillating topics. Lay it on thick, but not so thick that it becomes creepy. Instead, give it a little juice by rubbing her life line (the central line that curves down her palm near the thumb) while giving her these lines. That line is ticklish, and with the right combination of touch and suggestion you can send that tingle right up her arm and down her spine.

While this is basically a ruse, it can be useful to know a few things about palmistry before trying to predict her future (which I suspect points to her ending up with you). For that information, you may wish to consult a book on palmistry, such as *Palm Reading: A Little Guide to Life's Secrets*, by Dennis Fairchild or *Palm Reading for Beginners: Find the Future in the Palm of Your Hand*, by Richard Webster.

Initiating a Conversation

Whatever your approach—whether a simple one or a complicated gimmick—the first words out of your mouth are the bridge that takes you from no lines to friendly conversation. The key to the approach then, is to ask a question that will get her into conversation. This doesn't mean that your first words should be a question—you can always go with a joke or line—but you can never let it dangle without something to prompt her to respond. Remember, seduction is about positive interaction. The sequence is:

1. Use an opener (see The First Words out of Your Mouth, The Pick-up Line and Gimmicks portions) to initiate contact.
2. *Immediately* follow it with an open-ended question or, in other words, a question that she'll have to answer with more than a yes or no. Open-ended questions usually begin with "what" or "how".
3. Have at least one other open-ended follow-up question in mind, and preferably more, so that you don't stall out.
4. After three questions, provided her answers and your questions are interesting enough, you will be in conversation.

Chump File: Should I Ask for Her Name?

This may come as a surprise to you, but the answer is, "No!" Asking for her name might seem like an innocent and easy way of getting to know each other, but since everyone and his brother is doing it, this move is just plain lame. Just like your name doesn't tell her anything about you, her name doesn't tell you anything about her, so in essence it is just a useless piece of information. Useless and dangerous, so never volunteer to tell her your name either. If she's not yet interested, she'll just forget it. And if she is interested, believe me, she's going to ask for it. If, in the middle of a conversation, she suddenly says something like, "Oh my gosh, I don't even know your name," that is the clearest sign you could possibly get that you are making good progress. Even better, you've taken a position of power. She's the one asking for your name. She's the one eager to get to know you better—in all the right ways. As you'll learn later, it's always better to have a woman give you her phone number or invite you over *without you asking for it*. The same concept works here.

Some may argue that getting a name personalizes the encounter, that it's like being formally introduced. But does that mean that now that she knows your name, that you've been "introduced," she'll be burning hot for you? Hardly. It's much more likely you're getting formally categorized as a chump or, even worse, *a friend*.

One more argument against asking for names: you ask for her name and then, oh my gosh, you forget it! She expects you to know it but you don't, and now you're screwed, but not in the way you intended. If this happens, you've got to turn it back on her and make it seem like her name wasn't worth remembering. Try something like this, with a nonchalant, almost egotistical air, "I know you had a beautiful

> name . . . but what was it exactly?" This may save your ass,
> but my question is, why did you set yourself up for this prob-
> lem in the first place?
>
> In other words, names are fine as long as she initiates the
> exchange. Until then, remain a man of mystery.

At point 1, she's just surprised that you're talking to her. At point 2, you're still a stranger and the woman is wary. But by point 3, she'll have more or less accepted you and dropped her barriers. All this in a matter of a minute or two.

Of course, try a few approaches and you'll realize there are two kinds of women in the world: talkers and listeners. If she's a talker, it's easy—paraphrase her answers and turn them into relevant, intelligent questions right back to her. Of course, you shouldn't bombard her with a series of random questions that will make her feel as if she's at an interview—try to listen to what she's saying and have a *relevant* question ready. If she's a listener, you'd better have *two* good follow-up questions in mind, and a good conversation to fall back on, otherwise you're going to crash and burn (which is, of course, just another experience to learn from and use to tighten your game).

Pacing Her Ongoing Reality

Pacing her ongoing reality is the best tool to create instant rapport and make a connection. It's the approach I use most often, and it's the one I'd recommend to you, too, especially if you're a beginner.

The secret here is that you're actually going to talk to her about what's happening right at the moment—in other words that she's sitting in a bar, restaurant, train station, coffee shop, gym, etc.—as well as the fact that you're talking to her. She can't disagree with that, can she? And that's when you take it to the next level . . .

Chump File: Should I Buy Her a Drink?

I'll make it short and sweet: don't buy her a drink. Ever. Don't offer to buy her a drink. Don't agree to her demands ("I'm thirsty . . ." – "Will you buy me a drink?" etc.)—here's why: if you do, you supplicate. You're giving her the power, and women have nothing but scorn and disrespect for powerless men. Besides, you never want to create the expectation that you're going to buy things for her. You're not her bank. As I always say, gifts (dates, drinks, etc.) are rewards for sex that has *already taken place*. And don't forget it.

When a woman asks for a drink, here's what she's really thinking:

Her (*thinking, "Let's see if I can hook this sucker . . ."*): Will you buy me a drink?

You (*thinking, "Oh boy, am I in luck, this woman must like me!"*): Sure!

Her (*thinking, "Ha! What a wimp. Does he really think I'm gonna go to bed with him for a bottle of beer? Jeez . . . I'll take my drink and continue searching for a Real Man"*): Thanks! You're so sweet! Bye now!

You (*confused*): Hey . . . wait! Um . . . ?

If she stays for five or ten minutes and has a nice little chit-chat with you, that just means she's a nice person and the kind of woman you should have gotten to know *in the right way*. But forget it, this encounter is already over. You got off on the wrong foot by being an AFC and bowing to her power play, so she's already crossed you out in her book of prospective partners.

Offering to buy her a drink is even worse. Now you are voluntarily becoming a desperate, AFC-style supplicator. The woman will either refuse the drink (she wants nothing to do with a wimp like you), accept the drink and then ignore you (she still wants nothing to do with a wimp like you, but she wants the drink) or, if she has pity for your spinelessness, she'll stay and chat with you for a while. But don't be fooled. It's a pointless and rather uncomfortable conversation to be having, because the whole time she's thinking, *I accepted the drink, so I guess I should stay for a while because it would be rude to leave. But he's probably thinking that, since I'm staying, there's more in this for him. But there isn't! He's a supplicator! I don't want him! I'll have to try to make my exit the moment the situation presents itself.* In other words, no matter how much you talk, you don't stand a chance. Of course, you can turn the situation around if you're really good—but if you *were* really good, you wouldn't be in the situation in the first place!

So, what to do if she gives you the old "Buy me a drink" routine? Easy. Tell her no. That way you throw the ball back in her court, and you find out a little bit more about what she's really after. If she's just fishing for drinks and does not really care who she gets them from, she'll take the hint and move on to some chump down the bar. Good riddance! You did not need to waste any time on that woman.

On the other hand, she may be genuinely interested in you, and her opener is just the reverse of that popular AFC-line "Can I buy you a drink?" In that case, explain to her that it's against your principles to buy a strange woman a drink, but she should feel free to buy *you* a drink. An example:

Her: I'm thirsty. Could you buy me a drink?

You: Sorry, I don't buy drinks for women I don't know. But you could buy us both a drink, and then I could reciprocate once we get to know each other.

Her (thinking, "Argh . . . Gmph . . . He didn't supplicate!

Could this be . . . a real man? What's this, I'm getting wet!?"): Ah . . . um . . . Okay!"

The final circumstance is a case where she's clearly into you—you've been having a great conversation—and she uses the "buy me a drink" line to test you. This is very important, because it's going to define the relationship. Yes, she expects the drink as a sign of affection, and you need to affirm her belief that you're loving her company—but to buy her something now would be a major mistake. Remember, she may be hinting, but she hasn't given you anything yet, and drinks are only rewards for past behavior. In this case, step up to the plate and knock that ball right back to her—stronger than she pitched it to you.

Her: I like you. Will you buy me a drink?
You: Give me a French kiss.

Note that the tongue play is an explicit part of the bargain *up front*. None of this peck on the lips crap, because that isn't worth a paper umbrella, much less a whole drink. Here's the best part: you avoid being negative, and you turn it right back on her. You don't have to be the "jerk" for turning her down. Instead, she denied you . . . so now she has to make it up to you, or risk losing your interest.

If she says yes, make that the longest and sexiest French kiss she's ever had . . . and try for a few follow-up tonguings while you're at it. Then get her a drink as a reward for this very explicit action. Even if she's into the concept, she may hesitate before giving in. After all, this woman has class, so she doesn't want to appear too easy (yet). That's fine, because it gives you a chance to show personality and be playful. Give her a little guilt—"You aren't uptight are you? We're just having fun!"; "It's not hot sex or anything . . . just a little kiss!"—and she'll usually play along.

In practical terms, pacing the ongoing reality works like this. First, you describe the very recent past—the fact that just ten seconds ago she was sitting idly in this place. This is demonstrably true, so there's no way she can disagree with you. Plus, you've turned the conversation to her and shown that you are attentive. Even better, this is incredibly easy to do—you're just describing the scene, after all—and it doesn't involve any pick-up lines or other canned strategy (or so it seems). In other words, you've personalized this pick-up just for her.

Next, you describe the ongoing reality—the fact that you approached her and are talking to her right now. Again, this is something she can't possibly disagree with because it's true. You are standing right there talking to her. You are also talking with her in a humorous and pleasant manner. In other words, you are creating an atmosphere of honesty, simplicity, and enthusiasm for the moment. You are also drawing a connection between each other. You are both here in this place, and you are talking about the fact that you are talking, so you *must* have something in common. In other words, a connection.

Finally, you describe the near future events—the fact that she feels good and will continue to feel good about meeting a handsome stranger like yourself. This is the kicker. You've built rapport by telling her stuff that is clearly true, and now you're subtly switching to suggesting something you want to be true. She's agreed with you on several things already, so she is likely to agree with a few more questionable things (such as that fact that you're handsome and that she's happy you approached her) than she would have if you said them right from the start. You've made her re-evaluate her emotions in the context of your honesty and sincerity, and once she's thinking about your positive qualities, you're well on your way to success.

But be subtle. Don't overload her with things she probably won't agree with, and don't rush to the third step if you haven't nailed down the first two. Keep a balance between truth and suggestions, always pushing her "reality" a bit past the actual in a positive direction. If you push too hard she'll simply stop agreeing with you . . . and then bye-bye rapport, bye-bye love.

Stop in the Name of . . . Lust

Ross Jeffries (www.seduction.com) gives us the following example of pacing the ongoing reality. As usual with Jeffries, this is an extreme example that should only be used by experts.

Apparently, Jeffries lives near a bicycling, rollerblading, and jogging path, and, of course, he's developed a technique for taking advantage of this hot babe–intensive area—and no, he doesn't actually do any physical activity in this pick-up zone. Instead, he stands by the side of the path, and when he sees a pretty girl he jumps in her way and yells, "Stop!"

At this point, the woman is thinking he's completely nuts, so Jeffries uses that reality. First, he says he saw her jogging, biking, or blading (clearly true) and just wanted to meet her (obviously true, since he threw himself in her path). Now, clearly this is a crazy way to meet women, and the woman is no doubt thinking that, so Jeffries paces that ongoing reality by saying, "Look, I know this is a totally nutty way to meet people (exactly what I was thinking, she says to herself), but I knew that if I didn't do something to stop you, we'd never have a chance to talk (clearly true as well) and maybe see how much we really like each other (embedded suggestion)."

Obviously, Jeffries's technique here is a little extreme. He already has the confidence to make a scene, which all beginners and even most experienced PUAs lack. He also rushes quickly through the first two steps to the third in one sentence. In a normal situation, the first two steps could take up to a minute. And instead of suggesting openly that she is happy to be with you, he embeds this suggestion in another sentence (in other words, he has said "we really like each other" within the context of his sentence, hoping her unconscious mind will pick it up and start influencing her conscious thinking).

These embedded suggestions are part of Jeffries' Speed Seduction® technique, a short primer of which will also appear later in this book. Embedded suggestion is not needed to pace her ongoing reality; however, I mention this pick-up here because the concept is sound: get her attention by pointing out the circumstances, pace her ongoing reality by acknowledging her feelings, and then suggest that she is attracted to you and wants to get to know you better. If you've created rapport in the first two steps, this suggestion is probably your most powerful pick-up tool.

Kinesthetics

Words are powerful, but there's something even more powerful that is always at your disposal: touch. Whenever you are in a seduction situation, you should always touch the woman as often as possible. Or, as LordGaeden puts it on ASF: "Are there any clues as to when it's the right time to go kino? The clue is whenever it's possible (i.e., when she's within range)." In other words, if you can physically reach her, you should be touching her.

Now let me make something *perfectly clear:* I am talking about non-sexual, non-threatening touching. Never grope a girl, "accidentally" touch her private parts, or force yourself on her. That's not only gross and demeaning, it's criminal. You can and should be thrown in jail for that.

With kino, your goal is not to "get a piece," but to simply reinforce your connection with some physical contact. Psychological studies show that casual touching during a friendly conversation causes people to remember the conversation more fondly; so get to touching—and don't waste any opportunities.

The first thing you should do when you approach a girl is to kino her . . . by shaking her hand! This is an absolutely expected gesture, and a great source of first contact. Be firm but don't squeeze, and always hold the handshake longer than expected.

This will make her notice and think about the touch, without creeping her out.

If you already know the woman, for instance she's with a friend of yours or you've met her before, always hug her in greeting. Do not fall all over her. This will make you look like a fool or a pervert (not good, my friend), and cause her to become self-conscious and embarrassed. Understand the situation and use your best judgment. Sometimes a hug is a full chest-to-chest press; other times, it's just putting your arm around her shoulder and pulling her close for a moment.

Kino is also a vital tool to reinforce your come-on. If you say something to her and she responds positively at all, even with a momentary smile, touch her lightly on the hand or arm. This is a sexual advance, but a very subtle and intimate one. More importantly, you are reinforcing her positive feeling with a warm touch. If she responds positively (or not at all), feel free to brush something out of her hair or off her shoulder (and no, something doesn't actually have to be there). If you're really bold, go ahead and "brush an eyelash" off her cheek. These are all very delicate, sensitive maneuvers. Even better, they're the kind of things people do for each other when they're intimate, so you're reinforcing that personal bond.

The most important thing to remember with kino is to *pay attention to how she responds*. If she's comfortable with the non-sexual touching, then gradually get more sexual. She will either follow you straight into a make-out session, or she will tell you to stop when the contact gets so intimate it makes her uncomfortable. This is a mixed signal; if she's been positive up until now, the chances are that she likes the feeling of the kino, but she feels you're going too fast. In this case, go back to the basic non-sexual hand and arm touching. If she doesn't tell you to stop, you're well on your way.

If she tells you to stop again, by all means stop touching her and respect her space. Some women love to be touched (I call them "kino girls," and I discuss them more in the dancing section); some women feel it's a serious invasion of their personal space. They may be very attracted to you, and love what you're

Kino-ing Your Way from Friend to Fuck

Being the "nice guy" is for losers, because you're just going to end up being her "friend" instead of her bed buddy. This is not where you want to be—most of the time. There are a few PUAs who work the friend angle successfully, and their secret is kino.

The problem with being a nice guy is that you are non-threatening, weak, neutral, and non-sexual. Clearly, major turnoffs. But that's where kino comes in. As a nice guy, you are safe, so touching and hugging is obviously also safe. Before she knows it (or in other words, in a month), touching you will move from feeling good to feeling exciting to feeling electrifying. And that's when you've got her.

The key is to start kino-ing her from the very beginning, so that she's always expecting your touch. If you try to start after the relationship has started, she'll think you're trying to deliberately move from friend to fuck, and that's just not going to fly. You have to make the evolution seem natural, to slowly move along the chain and make her think it's *her* idea to move the relationship into the sexual realm.

Even better, once you've established that kind of flirty relationship with one friend, it's easy to establish it with all your female "friends." They see you touching another woman and it's social proof that the behavior is acceptable and non-threatening—and even better, it's fun.

Sounds great, right? Well, it's not. Being the nice guy is never the smart way to go. For one thing, this technique takes months of hard work to come to fruition. Meanwhile, she's probably going to be swept off her feet by some sexually charged, confident PUA. Then she'll come bragging (or crying) to you, her friend, with the details.

So, never intentionally fall into the friend trap. But if you do, remember that kino may still be your ticket out—if you start early enough and if you never forget to be physical.

saying, but are very private about being touched (until you're *in private* that is). Always respect her feelings, and never force anything with kino. I simply can't stress that enough.

Fun and Games

Here are a few games that are fun to throw down on a few women . . . and are likely to lead to even more fun. These aren't for your everyday routine, but they can be very useful in the right situation.

The Kissing Bet

Tell the girl that you are already getting friendly with (very important) that you will bet her a dollar that you can kiss her without using your lips or your tongue. This sounds like a come-on, so it might take some convincing. If she doesn't go for it, try the subtle approach. "Okay, fine . . . but check out this trick. You really can use it to make money off people." Play it off like a favor, which it is—to both of you. Once she agrees, move in like you are going to kiss her on the lips . . . pause . . . and lay the smoothest, and I mean the smoothest, kiss on her she has ever experienced. If she doesn't kiss you back, say, "I'm sorry, I couldn't resist. I guess I owe you a fuck. I mean a buck." If she seemed into it, say, "Nice, but only worth fifty cents. You owe me another one."

Truth or Dare

One internet poster got the idea of playing truth or dare when he saw that it could have some real—and really exciting—results. He asked a girl whether she had ever had a lesbian experience. The poster claimed that

> She told me that the only time was in a crazy game of truth or dare when she got dared to eat some girl out for five minutes. Neither of these girls was bi before it happened. This just goes to show that the possibilities are endless!
>
> —Anonymous Post, ASF

Truth or Dare is such a classic game that every boy over the age of fifteen has probably played it—or at least wet dreamed about playing it—with every girl he could find. In order to get a group of women to play this game, at least one of them has to be interested in getting a little freaky with someone from your group. Perfect, because after this game they're *all* going to be interested in getting freaky.

The key to a good game of Truth or Dare is to be prepared. Discuss with your friends who wants to be doing who by the end of the night, and prep each other with good truths and dares. And make sure you have all the right accessories, such as whipped cream and carrots (for fake blow jobs). You will be amazed how hot a girl can get just from having whipped cream licked off her stomach.

The best part about truth or dare is that you can really get into the kinky stuff that's a little awkward to bring up in polite conversation (or even impolite bed talk). It's best to let the women open the door to the sexual stuff (they will if one of their friend's wants you or one of your friends), so start with a few non-sexual tricks. Then move into the kissing, followed by the whipped cream, lap dances, lesbian action, and anything else you can think of. The game ends only after everyone is hot and heavy—the sign of which is the girls making you do randy things to them. Dare your wingman (not the girl!) to go into the next room with his girl for five minutes. Hopefully, for all of you, he does not return.

The King

A Japanese version of Truth or Dare that is slightly superior because random luck—and not the intent of the player—determines who will be dared. In fact, it's possible that you will never be dared, which frees you to really get crazy on your friends (or so the logic goes) because you don't have to worry about the eventual retribution.

Chump File

Can't handle the honest approach, or even a cheesy gimmick? Well, here's an AFC-style approach that's difficult to attempt and not very effective either! It's from an anonymous contributor to Mindlist, and I'd remain anonymous too if I was giving this sort of advice. Learn from this, my friends, that deception is no easier than the truth—and much more confusing.

The anonymous contributor advocates knocking on her door, holding a shoe or sock or something. When she answers the door, he holds up the shoe, tells her that he found it while he was passing by and asks if it belongs to her (as I said, I'd remain anonymous if I gave this advice). When she says no, he smiles and says that he guesses that it must belong to him. He then starts chatting, and even sits down. At this point, the woman will either laugh and invite him in or ask what he's doing (and possibly call the cops). At this point, he says that he is getting tired and wants to rest so that he can put more energy into making her laugh.

Mind-numbing approaches like this are ultimately better than doing absolutely nothing, since the only true failure is the failure of not even trying. And you never know, you might even get lucky every once in a while. Then again, you might also get lucky by knocking at her door and asking her outright whether she'd fancy a shag. In fact, studies have shown that one out of twenty-five to thirty so-called "cold approaches" (just asking a stranger to have sex with you) will get a positive response. So the chance is there (hovering around the 3–4 percent mark), but compared to all the other and better things you could try with her, they are just too damn slim.

The game goes like this: on the count of three, everyone extends their hands with a number of fingers out. The fingers are added up, and then the players are counted counter-clockwise from the last "King" (or if the game just started, from the person who suggested the game in the first place). The person who ends up with the final number is the "King" and the person who gets to dare. Once the "King" has decided what the dare is, the same process of finger pointing and counting is repeated. The "King" is excluded from this count (although there is a variation where the "King" may end up with his own dare, so just make sure you agree upon the rules beforehand). This time, the person who ends up the final number is the one who will be dared. No awkwardness; no hurt feelings. It's just the luck of the draw (or the fingers).

An alternate version can also be played where the "King" gets to choose whoever he or she wants to dare. Now that's power!

Your Last Chance

If you've tried two or three unsuccessful approaches with a woman and are already pretty certain that this seduction isn't going to end up between the sheets or even with a fake phone number, but you're really into the challenge or into this specific woman for some reason (and we're talking about a seduction here, not some kind of soul mate or special person) then there's one more thing you can try: be rude.

That's right, just start cutting in on her and then ignoring her, only to butt in and say something rude again when the next chance arises. If she asks why, just tell her it's nothing personal, you're just having some fun and doing what you want. She might just have a change of heart and start making passes at you. Just keep ignoring her and pushing her away; it will make her crazy, and if she keeps at it (and you keep your cool and keep being rude), you'll eventually be able to do whatever you want with her. Remember, though, that this is absolutely a last resort. If it doesn't work, well, she was on her way out anyway. But it may be that she turns out to be the kind of girl that likes, wants, and needs a little kick in the ass every once in a while in order to develop respect for a man—and then the rude approach will hit the jackpot for you.

The Secret of Success: Persistence and a Smile

Approaches are a dime a dozen, and there are far more out there than you could ever hope to find, not to mention try. The approaches and lines in this book only scratch the surface and mainly serve as a guide to helping you find your own personal style.

But that leaves one question unanswered, and this is one I hear all the time: What is the most important element of the approach? The answer is . . . to smile. Now, you may be tempted right now to think back to some of the non-smiling ladies' men you may have known, but let me remind you, even the classic stone-faced Humphrey Bogart had his smirk, which almost always proved to be the breaking point for women.

A smile not only lets the woman know you're having fun and not taking yourself too seriously, it shows that you're a fun guy to get to know. And it's contagious. If you keep smiling, she'll find it harder and harder to keep from smiling herself. And once she's smiling, you've got your foot in the front door.

Don't believe in the power of a smile? Sounds too simple? I think this story from NightLight9 helps illustrate the point:

> Early in the evening, he notices a girl. She is attractive, but clearly with another guy. Now she is sitting with a group of girlfriends at a table. He makes eye contact with her and waves for her to come over to him, but, of course, she isn't going to fall for that, and remains with her friends. He slowly walks over to her and sits down, as close to her as he can. She is giving off as cold a vibe as possible, but he does not let that distract him. He asks her why she's at the bar,

but he keeps a huge smile on his face. He keeps up the simple, even boring, questions, but he keeps an enormous grin on his face while they talk.

After a few openers, he asks her what she does for a living, but he interrupts before she can answer, saying, "No wait—let me guess. You're a lion tamer." She doesn't smile, but she's clearly interested. He asks her questions about lion taming—does she crack the whip, does she stick her head in the lion's mouth, is the risk exciting? Even though she still hasn't smiled, she's going along with the game. Then she lets her ankle brush his leg. His smile grows wider, and he puts his hand on her knee. As they continue to talk, he moves a little closer. He gives her a quick kiss, then another, longer, kiss. The man she was with earlier comes back, and our PUA smiles and acts friendly to him (he knows, after all, who she's going home with). A few minutes later, she tells the man that she's leaving with NightLight9. Our PUA says, "The only way to defeat the bitch shield is with a smile (and lots of eye contact)."

And that, my soon-to-be-successful friend, is advice you can take to the bank—and to bed.

The Foreigner from Hell: If He Can Do It, Anybody Can!

Persistence is so important that I wanted to include the ultimate example. You should learn a few valuable lessons from it. The first lesson is that looks really don't matter and the second is that persistence pays. It's not the guys who don't get rejected that succeed, it's the guys who take a knock and get back on their feet that wind up with the beautiful women.

I can remember seeing countless guys, ugly guys, hustling their hearts out with clearly no chance of success . . . until I saw them at the end of the night with a beautiful woman on their arm. The best story I know, however, is one told by famed PUA Maniac, and is called "The Foreigner from Hell."

The story begins in a Tokyo club. Maniac is working the crowd when he spots, over in the distance, a short, fat foreigner who is "ugly as sin, wearing clothes that look like they came from the Salvation Army . . . he was forty-five years old and . . . probably had a shit job taking chicken guts out of a bird in a processing plant." Needless to say, this guy was by far the most pathetic chump in the club.

So what did he do? He went out on the dance floor and hit on every single woman in the club! He started with the most beautiful women, and one by one, they all blew him off. He worked his way down the chain until he had hit on every girl in the club. Every single girl in the place had just rejected him! So what did he do? *He started again at the top with the most beautiful women!* Not once but at least twice, he worked his way down the line, and he just didn't give up. As long as he got a reaction, either positive or negative, he kept on hitting, getting rejected, and coming back for more punishment.

The guy finally started dancing with an attractive woman who had blown him off ten minutes (and twenty pick-up attempts) before. At first, she resisted, giving him really bad looks—remember this guy was ugly as a bucktoothed hound dog—but then she started to relax. He took it slow, kept making advances, and attempting kino. Initially, she pushed every advance away, but he never got discouraged. Over time, she got more relaxed—she allowed more nonsexual touching, closed her eyes and really enjoyed dancing, and eventually started to permit some more sensual touching—and twenty minutes later, they were kissing all over each other!

To make a long story short, The Foreigner from Hell left the club with a beautiful, twenty-something Japanese woman that night! If he can get that kind of action, anyone, and I mean *anyone*, can get action. So you see, it's all about confidence, personality, and the "reality" you create with your actions.

So stop making excuses already. Get out there and approach!

CHAPTER **4**

GM Style

Grand Master Style Explained

Grand Master style (known as GM) is an advanced technique that takes an extraordinary amount of self-control and the kind of outgoing personality that allows you to just keep talking without getting flustered—even if the woman is glaring you down or trying to slap you. The technique originated with a Paris-based PUA known only as Grand Master and was first described to the world by fellow PUA Nathan Szilard.

Grand Master style is based on continuous smutty jokes and humorous sex-talk with keen attention to how the girl reacts. To begin, start by telling a girl flat out in no uncertain terms that you want to fuck her. Yes, that's the first thing you say to her! Needless to say, most girls will react negatively (some even violently) when first approached with GM style, so it's important to defuse the situation by keeping up your chatter and not letting her get in a single word. You do this by quickly following up your original "let's get busy" come-on with a "just kidding, just kidding!" Then, before she can react to either your first statement or the "apology," deliver another smutty statement and a joke.

And after each of those, quickly mop up with "just kidding" and, ideally, with an apologetic hug. If she doesn't walk away in disgust within the first minute, you'll dirty talk her right into bed.

The genius here is that you're accomplishing all the things a PUA should do and be in any pick-up situation—you're honest about your intentions, you're acting as the dominant male, you're confident and in control of the situation, you're funny and using kinesthetics (touching) and sexual talk to get her thinking about sex. And because the girl has no chance to respond negatively to your comments, she's unconsciously starting to accept what is being said. She is simply not given a chance to protest because of your constant barrage of smutty remarks, jokes, and the quick "just-kidding, I'm sorry, let me hug you" follow-up. Unconsciously, though, she is only seeing herself *not* protesting; therefore, she must be accepting what is being said, right? Not really, but don't tell her that!

Even better, she's imagining all these sexual scenarios in your jokes and remarks and, while she may be repelled at first, her defenses will eventually go down, her mind will start to race, and before you know it, her imagination is going wild and she's getting horny like never before.

The GM style is aggressive. Basically, using the GM style, you're telling a woman that you want to fuck her the first time that you meet her. The genius is that the woman sees your attitude. She knows that you feel you can satisfy her sexually and that you have confidence. It is easy to believe that women don't want sex—but they are horny too! The GM style allows a PUA to put the idea of sex right in front of a woman, and to get her mind thinking of sex with you (even if you aren't her first choice, you're the one offering sex to her).

Obviously, this is high-risk territory. You must be extremely confident and proficient to pull off a GM-style pick up. If you stumble, if you stutter, if you forget your next line or hesitate and let her say something sassy and negative back to you, you will get bitch-slapped. Hard.

> ### No Guilt, No Shame
>
> Make no mistake, GM style is uncomfortable and embarrassing, especially for a beginner. If your target turns out to be a dirty girl, good for you! But what if she's a nice girl, a real sweetheart? Don't give up! If she wasn't into your act, she'd walk away. If she's blushing and being shy, that's actually a very positive sign. Always remember, once you start GM style on a girl, you can never go back. If it doesn't work, it doesn't work, but never try to change style mid-stream. You'll only lose the girl—and your self-respect.

GM Style: Level Two

Once you've got your basic GM patter down, it's time to take your act to the next level and really start playing with her mind. Here are a few techniques—let's just call them exploratory riffs on the basic GM approach—that will push the woman further out of her comfort zone, and (hopefully) into a sexual frenzy.

Neg her negative. Sometimes the girl is too quick for you and follows your initial volley of filthy innuendo with a negative comment, or maybe with a rude gesture. If you're going to save this encounter, you have to be fast and aggressive. Cut her down with a quick, "Hey, I'm just trying to have some fun. I didn't know you were against fun." She's being negative, but you're throwing that right back in her face and making it seem that she's the one with the attitude problem, not you. Now she has to prove to you that she *is* fun, by either accepting—or even one-upping—your smutty banter! We'll learn more about negging in the next chapter.

Compliment yourself. Make sure your banter always refers back to how wonderful you are for her. For instance, constantly talking about your huge penis is a classic GM-style maneuver, because you're not only being smutty and making her think about sex, you're making her think about how wonderful sex would be *with you*. It doesn't matter how big your penis actually is, because by the time she sees it, it's highly unlikely that she will change her mind. More importantly, girls don't really care about penis size! When she wants it, she just wants it. Besides, you *are* going to satisfy her sexually. That's a PUA guarantee, and you need to make *sure* you deliver on it by being attentive to her needs in bed.

Call her a slut. Most AFC go the blubbering "you're beautiful" route, which we all know by now is usually a huge mistake. With GM style, you can turn things around by insisting that she's being provocative and sexually forward. Just keep saying stuff like, "I can't believe you're looking at me like that, you are such a slut," or "You don't even know you're doing it, that's how much of a slut you are." This serves a dual purpose. First, it negs her, which, as we'll learn, is a powerful tool in the right circumstances. Second, it turns her into the aggressor. Is she really being slutty and flirty? Probably not, but you're making her *believe* that she is—and once you've got her convinced of that, it's just a short jump to her acting on that belief with you.

Quote her something naughty. You want to tell her to get down on her knees and suck you right now? Better not. But you could put that request into the context of story you've been told. For instance, here's a story from an anonymous poster on ASF, which you can present with something like, "Can you believe what happened to my buddy's sister yesterday?" You begin: "My buddy's sister was standing by herself in a bar when this guy walks up to her, looks her dead in the eyes, and said, 'I would like to fuck you. Would you like to fuck me?' and then just stands there. She said she nearly dropped her drink, but then she started to think about it and began feeling that heat build up in her body. You know how you feel when you start to get really aroused? All wet and excited? She didn't miss a beat and started playing right back at him. She said, 'I'd want you to go down on me first.' He didn't blink an eye, and he took it from there, nego-

---

**The Cave Man Approach
(For Those Too Lazy to Even Try)**

A friend of mine has a minimalist GM technique that seems to work. He simply grunts sex to women. That's it! Seems to work about ten percent of the time . . . he rarely leaves a bar or party empty-handed.

—David Off, ASF

---

tiating the sexual encounter until they were both so hot that they left together."

Now, supposedly, this really happened. But you know what's even better? Now you can tell this story to a woman in a bar, while looking her dead in the eye. You can tell her exactly what you want her to do, but you're protected because you're just telling her the story your buddy told you!

GM-Style Openers and Lines

Here's a pocketful of GM pick-up lines to keep you going for at least a little while. Remember that GM style is all about using one line (or joke or story) right after another, so you'll need a bunch of these for every seduction situation. So, here they are:

- "I can't please every girl, but I'll give you the chance of a lifetime tonight."
- "Nice shoes. Wanna fuck?"
- "It's tough being a sex symbol."
- "You aren't going to get too horny if I sit next to you, are you?"
- "I like the look of your crotch."
- "You should stare at the floor for a while [*pause*], because I'm going to have you staring at the ceiling for a week."
- "I'm organizing an orgy for my friend's birthday. Want to come?" (which she hears as, "Wanna cum?")

- "The word of the day is legs. Let's go back to my place and spread the word."

- "Let's go back to my place, order some pizza, and fuck. Hey, just kidding! We can order Chinese instead."

- "I like you because you're intelligent (*gesture to her breasts*). I like myself because I'm intelligent, too (*gesture toward your crotch*)."

- "I like your legs so much I'm going to name them. This one is Christmas and this one is New Years. Can I see you between the holidays?"

- "Do you know the difference between a hamburger and a blow job? No? Then let's do lunch sometime."

- "Look, I have a date in two hours, so we better go to your place now."

- "I don't believe in sex without mutual consent. And oh, by the way, you have my consent."

- "Ever tried one of those weird prickly condoms?"

- Her: "Do you mind if I smoke?" You: "Why should you be any different than all the other women I have sex with?"

- "Pardon me. Are you a screamer or a moaner?"

- "I have to go to the hospital tomorrow to get an operation (*point at your crotch*). Mine's too big."

- "Do you know how I can have a twelve-inch dick? Fold it in half."

- "I want to be appreciated for who I am, not just my huge dick."

- "Can you help me? I have to pee and the doctor says I can't lift anything heavy."

- "Why don't you sit on my lap and we'll talk about the first thing that pops up."

- "Do you wake up early in the morning? Her: Not unless I have to. You: Good, I don't like to be disturbed when I'm asleep."

GM-Style "Dirty" Jokes

A few longer pieces to keep the ball rolling. Memorize at your own risk!

Pants in the Air Hey girls, do you know how you can tell whether you liked us? "No," they reply. Well tonight, when you get home, remove your panties and throw them at the ceiling. If they stick, that means you liked us!

The Telepathic Watch A man walks into a bar and takes a seat beside a beautiful woman. He gives her a quick glance, then casually looks at his watch. The woman asks, "Is your date running late?" "No," he replies, "I just bought this state-of-the-art watch and was testing it." "Oh, yeah? What's so special about it?" "It uses alpha waves to telepathically talk to me," he explains. "Well, what's it saying now?" "It says you're not wearing any panties." The woman giggles and replies, "Well, it must be broken then, because I'm wearing panties." The man taps the watch's face for a second, then looks up and says, "Damn thing must be an hour fast!"

Doctor's Appointment One night, as a couple lay in bed, the husband gently tapped his wife on the shoulder and started rubbing her arm. The wife turned over and said, "Sorry honey, I have a gynecologist appointment in the morning and want to stay fresh." A few minutes later, the husband rolled back over and tapped the wife again. This time he whispered in her ear, "Do you have a dentist appointment, too?"

Laying Off Mr. Smith owns a small business. He has two employees, Jack and Jill. They are both extremely good employees, but after going over the finances he realizes he has to lay one of them off. As he's contemplating this, he sees Jill rub her head, reach for a bottle of aspirin, take a pill from the bottle, and head for the water fountain. Mr. Smith, unhappy about the situation but resigned to the problem with his finances, follows her to the water fountain and taps her on the shoulder. "Jill," he says, "I'm going to have to lay you or Jack off." Sarah replies, "Could you jack off? I have a headache."

The Gift A young man wanted to purchase a gift for his sweetheart's birthday, since they had been dating for almost a year. After long consideration, he decided on a pair of gloves: romantic, but not too personal. Accompanied by his sweetheart's sister, who knew everything about style, he went to the store and bought the gloves. The sister decided to buy a pair of panties for herself. Unfortunately, the clerk got the packages mixed up in the wrapping, so the young man ended up sending his sweetheart the panties with this note:

> I chose these because I noticed you weren't in the habit of wearing any when we go out in the evening. If it had not been for your sister, I would have chosen the long ones, but she wears short ones that are easier to remove.
>
> These are a delicate shade, but the lady I bought them from showed me the pair she had been wearing for three weeks and they were hardly soiled. I had her try yours on, and she looked really good.
>
> When you take them off, remember to blow in them before putting them away, as they will naturally be a little damp from wearing.
>
> I wish I were there to see you put them on for the first time, as no doubt other hands will come in contact with them before I return.
>
> Just think, though, how many times I will kiss them during the coming year. I hope you will wear them for me on Friday night so I can do just that as soon as I see you.
>
> P.S. The latest style is to wear them folded down with a little fur showing.

One-Liners Easier to remember than the longer pieces, but not nearly as funny:

Q: Why is air a lot like sex?
A: Because it's no big deal unless you're not getting any.

Q: Why did Frosty the Snowman pull this pants down?
A: He heard the snow blower coming.

Q: What's the difference between light and hard?
A: You can sleep with a light on.

The Ideal Guy Routine

This isn't really GM style, but its sole purpose is to get a woman horny, so I've thrown it in here. It's called The Ideal Guy Routine. You can use it as a follow-up if you haven't been getting a response with your GM-style smut (positive nor negative), but this works perfectly well as a separate routine as well.

Just get direct with her and ask her about her ideal guy. Make her dig deep. If you can get her to think about things in more detail than she usually does, she'll usually latch onto this game with glee. Have her describe his clothes, hair, voice, what he says to her, how his chest feels, and how his arms feel around her. Then, if you want to push it farther, have her tell you what she'd do to seduce this fictional beau-hunk right here, right now.

This is harmless right? You're obviously not that ideal guy.

Think again. What you're doing, obviously, is getting her thinking about the guy she wants to fuck. Then she starts thinking about what that guy would feel like. Then what the experience would be like. She's getting horny thinking about this non-existent guy, and who is she talking to? You! You can get her to think about her ideal guy all night if you want. He's the fantasy, you're the real guy standing next to her, and she's getting ready to blow (pun intended).

Even better, sooner or later she will realize that it is actually you who is making her wet with your conversation, not dream boy. Her lust is built up to almost intolerable levels, she is in the mood she only thought she'd be with her dream guy, so she's looking for that release. And guess who she's talking with? That's right, you. And that's when she realizes that you're a man, that she trusts you, and that you've made her horny. Now take a wild guess who the lucky guy is going to be tonight.

CHAPTER **5**

Neg Hits

Neg Hits Explained

*"When you approach a gorgeous girl, she basically
knows you want to fuck her. You have to somehow
convey that you didn't come for sex. . . . The only
thing that can make a 'ten' notice you is if you
show her she doesn't matter to you in the
slightest . . . that is a neg."*

—Mystery

GM is a style, an attitude. I can't necessarily endorse it, but I know
it works if you have the right personality—and the right girls. In
general, though, it's more of a change-up to your normal routine,
something to keep you from getting bored when you're having
sex four, five, or six times a week with different beautiful women.

Neg hits (or negging), on the other hand, is a technique that
will truly take your seductions to the next level and make you
the killer stud you have always wanted to be. Right now, if
you're practicing what you've learned so far, you should already
be getting a lot of action from very good looking women—say
"eights" on a scale of one to ten. That's great, but why settle for
the hot chicks when you could be bedding down with the most

extraordinarily good-looking women on the planet, the model-level women that every guy dreams of? Sure, these women are pros at turning guys down and crushing their spirits, but you're different. You're irresistible—and it's all because of neg hits.

I've adopted this term, as well as this technique, from legendary PUA Mystery, so we should all bow down and worship him right now for providing us with this incredible tool for the most crucial of situations in the world of seduction—getting the absolute perfect "ten" women.

The secret of this technique is in understanding the psychology of the "ten." A perfect "ten" knows that she is beautiful. She gets complimented all the time (and there's always the mirror to confirm it). Even worse, she has AFCs coming up to her and drooling all over her, complimenting her beauty, trying to get with her by supplicating at least twenty times a day. She's desensitized to it, and the truth is even worse than that. An attractive woman is flattered by your come-on because she needs the ego boost; a gorgeous woman is annoyed by your come-on because she's hit on all the time. She is prepared to shoot you down in a ball of flames, and she's got the experience to do it in the most painful ways possible. She may accept your compliment, or even your offer to buy her a drink (if you're a total AFC and ignore everything I've taught you), but in the end she's going to brush you off like a flake of dandruff.

What you have to do is stand out from the drooling crowd. And the easiest way to do that is to make it perfectly clear *that you are not interested in her*. When you approach her or her group, or even if you're standing next to her in line, she is expecting a come-on from you. So don't give it to her. Instead, say something mildly insulting, then just kind of look away like you couldn't care less what she thinks. For instance, if you notice she has long nails that are probably fake, say "Nice nails. Are they real?" When she says, "No," you reply, "Oh, well I guess they still look good." Do not be cruel or deliberately hurtful. Instead, frame your comment as a compliment, and just keep smiling.

What you're doing is qualifying her. All the other guys who approach her have hard-ons; but she's failed to meet your expectations. It's not an insult; it's just a judgment call. You're a nice guy, you're interesting, you're happy to talk to her, but sorry, she's just not up to your sexual standards.

In essence, you've turned her world upside down. She may act annoyed when men hit on her, but in reality she knows that's the source of her power. When she's breaking hearts, she's in control. This kind of woman loves to be the center of attention—chances are she's gotten things her way all her life because that's how beautiful people live—and she's going to be desperate to get that control back.

Even better, she's curious about why you aren't hot for her. Obviously, you have really high standards. Are you *that* hot and successful? Or are you married? What's the deal? She just has to know.

At this point, she will try to turn you into every other guy that has ever come up to her. In other words, she will try to do damage control by getting you to fall for her. She'll probably neg you back with a vaguely insulting comment to show she is even less interested in you than you are in her. Don't believe her. This is called flirting. She's just trying to attract you, so she can crush you like she does every other bug with the nerve to approach her.

But, of course, you don't fall for it. You take her negs and just keep talking with her about some neutral topic. You don't get sexual, and you don't go into pick-up mode. Instead, you just stay "friendly," and, when the opportunity arises, you drop in another neg or two. Eventually, she will drop her bitch shield and start working to attract you—not in order to crush you, but in order to actually win you over.

After all, her self-confidence and position of power depends on her winning this battle. And, irony of ironies, that's exactly what you want to happen, too!

The Specifics of Negging

Negging is a delicate art. Push her too hard, and you can actually end up destroying her confidence. Don't neg her enough, and she'll turn on you and tear you apart. And you always have to make sure the situation is right before you start negging. This is a very situational technique, so always remember these simple guidelines:

- *Use negs on "nines" and "tens" only,* and preferably only on "tens." The woman's confidence has to be sky-high— they have to believe 100 percent that they are too good for you and every other man on the planet—or the neg will destroy their confidence and make them despise you. Remember, you're taking their power, and this is a very delicate operation.

- *Be sensitive to her reaction.* Even "nines and tens" some-times have low self-esteem. Also, if they're depressed or in a bad mood, they don't want to hear your subtle insults. In this case, you need to be bringing them up instead of putting them down.

- *Always present your neg as a compliment.* Be charming, friendly, positive, earnest, and sincere. If your neg sounds like a deliberate insult, you come off sounding like a jerk, and then she can dismiss you as a head case. What you want is for her to believe you are a nice, sin-cere man who *should* have the hots for her, but doesn't.

- *Never walk away from a neg.* More often than not, she will not follow you. Instead, subtly turn away and direct your attention elsewhere (preferably on another woman in her group, if it's a group situation). This gives her the opportunity to neg you back, without having to run after you. After all, you're standing right there.

- *Use your negs wisely.* You have to get as close to her breaking point as you can without pushing her over. A really snotty girl (high bitch shield) should get three negs in the first three minutes. A less snotty girl should get two over a longer period of time.

Once you've negged her into interest and gotten her to the breaking point, turn the conversation around and start appreciating things about her—her style, wit, attitude, or sense of humor. But never compliment her looks! That just drops you back into that dreaded AFC zone. You've gotten her to drop her shield and respect you as an equal. She's off her perch and back in standard seduction territory—and even better, you've already established a ton of rapport with her—so go ahead and seduce her already!

Neg Examples (Free for the Taking)

Here are some classic negs to get you started. Remember, though, that your neg should make sense in context. It's no use "complimenting" her nails if they're obviously not fake, or joking about her height if she's not trying to secretly boost it with ultra-high heels.

- "Is that a hairpiece? No? Well, it's neat. I don't see it a lot. What do you call that hairstyle—the waffle?"
- "Your dress is nice. . . . I think I've seen you around before and you were wearing it then, too."
- "What do you do?" She answers, "I'm a model." You then reply, "Oh, like a hand model or something?"
- "You're funny looking, but there's something about you that intrigues me. Sorry, I'm just being honest."
- When she's talking, say, "Oh . . . gross . . . you just spit on me."
- "You're kind of tall. I like tall women. Are those four- or five-inch heels you're wearing?"
- "Well, you have a great body . . . and that makes up for a lot of other things."
- "You blink a lot."
- "That is so funny, the way your nose wiggles when you talk."
- "I don't think we should get to know each other." She asks, "Why?" and you respond, "Well, you're just too much of a nice girl for me."

A Coffee Shop Pick-up

Here's an example based on a post by Svengali that demonstrates the power of both negging and GM style. In this case, the friend is the primary and Svengali's riding wingman (see Chapter 6, Group Situations, for more details). This scene goes down in a crowded coffee house in the middle of the day. And . . . action!

Friend: It's beautiful how you spread your legs when you sit, but it would be so much more beautiful with a short skirt.

Her: Excuse me? What makes you think you can talk to me that way?

Friend (with a smile on his face): Now you're angry because I'm enjoying the view! Just because I let you know how I'd like to have sex with you! Look around . . . how many women are here?

Her: About twelve.

Friend (pointing): Just look around. See that woman? She has a nice ass . . . nicer than yours. And see that woman? Her clothes are the hottest in here. And see her? Her face and legs are better than yours. I saw something in you that's better than what any woman here has, and you're angry that I'm pointing it out. It's gorgeous, but by wearing those pants, you're not letting anyone else enjoy it. What do you think, Svengali?

Svengali (smiling): I think you're right.

Needless to say, she was so blown away by this GM-style negging that she didn't know how to respond. And the long and short of it was, according to Svengali, that "we were both doing her about an hour and a half from the time we first met her." Which just goes to show, you never know what goodies are waiting for you, if you have the nerve.

CHAPTER **6**

Group Situations

The Wingman

"I think some guys purposely hang out with unattractive friends so they look like studs by comparison. It works against them—even if a guy is the best-looking of the bunch, it just makes me think he's the head nerd."

—Danielle, New Orleans

Going out scoping women with a friend or group of guys is practically a rite of passage for most American males. And it can be a huge help in picking up women, especially in a bar, nightclub, or other obvious pick-up scenes. First of all, it gives the women the right impression, which is that you're a fun-loving guy with friends. Second, it gives you something to do besides hanging out by yourself like a pathetic loser (or drunk) when you're not talking to women. Of course, you *should* be talking to women all the time, so this can become a crutch. So be careful; if you're going to use a friend, make sure he's not just an excuse for you to ignore the Three Second Rule and lose your spine.

You've also got to be careful about who you choose to associate with. As Danielle said in the above quote, hanging out with losers doesn't make you look good, it makes you look like the lead dork. You're much better off hanging out with good-looking guys. As I've always said, *your* looks don't really matter (although if your friend is just ridiculously handsome you may find some girls getting a little too distracted for their own good).

The key is to make sure that your friends are just like you: well-groomed, fun-loving males prepared to worship the Three Second Rule and primed to score some hot chicks. After all, you're sometimes going to break away from the group to talk to a girl one-on-one, but as often as not you're going to be approaching women with your friend by your side. That's why he's known as your wingman, because he's there to back you up in case you get in a tight spot. And since you're both players (or on your way), it's best to get the ground rules straight before you're chatting up the ladies.

1. Discuss every situation ahead of time, preferably even before entering the club or bar. Make sure you're working together, not against each other.

2. Know who's the primary and who's flying wing, and stick with the arrangement. He who spots the women and wants to approach is the primary. He opens the conversation, and he gets first crack at the woman of his choice (in a group situation). The wing either runs interference on the lust-object's friend (known as "the obstacle") or, if he's into her, runs his own game on the hot and saucy obstacle.

3. If you're the primary, one of the first things you must always do is introduce and compliment your friend (he's a great guy, he's my best friend, he's on a football scholarship to State U, etc.).

4. Never steal a woman your friend is talking to. If she's giving you the vibe, back away, and give him room to reel her back in. He'll know soon enough when the game is up . . . and then it's your turn. Besides, being a little mysterious is always the best way to get a woman.

The Two-on-Two Routine

Here's a classic routine when you're with a buddy and you see two beautiful women. Do I have to mention the Three Second Rule again at this point? I hope not.

1. Approach with a smile.
2. Introduce your wingman.
3. Praise and commend your wingman.
4. Compliment the girl as if you're speaking for your friend. This is actually a brilliant way to avoid the appearance of a come-on. Although you're the one saying the compliments, you're framing them as something your friend is thinking, so the girl can't conclude that you're coming on to her. On the other hand, she can't blame your friend for coming on to her either, since he isn't really doing anything except standing there. Since she has nobody specific to object to, she will only feel the positive side of being complimented and none of the negatives. This approach also completely relieves you of undue performance pressure, since the woman never even has a chance to pass judgment on you or your friend.
5. Every time you compliment her, touch her. ("My friend thinks you have nice hair . . ."—stroke her hair—". . . extremely feminine hands . . ."—hold her hands, etc.).
6. You're remembering to make eye contact, right?
7. Once you're holding her hands, say "He really likes you," and pass her off to him. The other girl (the obstacle) is probably either laughing, or just about to object, so subtly reach over and take her hand. Shoot her a little eye contact, like you've been in it for her all along.
8. High five your wingman.
9. Say to your girl, "He's great, isn't he?" If she doesn't pull away, you're in.

Remember, it's not the amount of time spent with the woman, but the quality of the time—and at the end of the night, that's what counts.

5. Never argue with a girl, ever, even if she's an obstacle trying to block your or your wingman's path.
6. Once your friend steps off, jump in immediately. That's right—three seconds, no more.

Remember, when a friend gets laid, especially if you helped him lock down the score, that's a positive. You should feel happy and proud, because you're a part of it. If you feel bitter, then you're a loser because you're forgetting the golden rule of being a PUA: there's always another fish out there just waiting to be hooked.

Besides, now he owes you one. The more action you land for friends, the more likely it is that a friend will go out of his way to help land action for you. The more that comes around, the more that goes around, my friend.

The Wingman Club

Johnny Shack, of merry old England, has suggested a rather interesting twist on the use of PUA partners, which I've dubbed The Wingman Club. It goes like this:

Get together with three to five friends ("mates" in ye olde British jargon) and start a club dedicated to each member getting one phone number for each other member per month. Believe me, with five guys you're going to be busy—what with five women to call and five numbers to get for your mates. With all this practice, you'll be a PUA in no time, if you're not already. Even better, you'll be approaching girls on behalf of your friend, so you'll be getting practice with women without getting the old ego bruised.

Be as straightforward in this exercise as possible. Just walk up to a beautiful woman (and, no, it's not funny to set your friend up with war-dogs, because he'll just return the favor to you—twice as bad), and say, "Hi, I noticed you a minute ago and . . . well, this might sound strange . . . (laugh here to set her off her guard and show that you're a good guy) . . . well, see . . . (don't sound rehearsed) . . . my friend just broke up with his girl-friend and he's a bit down. (Always give the impression you—or in this case your friend—has just broken up with a woman. It will keep women from thinking you're alone because there's something wrong with you. It's twisted, but it's true. This line works.) I told him to do something crazy and let me set him up on a blind date. Anyway, I think you're perfect for him. He's a great guy and very good looking. (It's vital to mention that he's cool and good-looking. Even if he's not, she'll hope it's true and create a positive association in her mind. And saying she's per-fect for him because he's good-looking . . . well, you're just stroking her ego, too.) How about you give me your phone number and I'll tell him to call you? If you like each other, you can go out."

You've given her the low-key approach, implying it's only a phone call. Still, she may ask for your friend's number instead of giving you hers, in which case you should say, "That sounds okay, but I know he has to go away for work soon (this implies he's not only gainfully employed, but also successful) and it's probably better if I give him your number. Is that okay?" The question is important because it shows you're not being pushy, that you really are just trying to find the most practical solution to the situation.

If she insists on calling him, just give her the number already—but give her a few parting shots about what a great guy he is to get her juices flowing.

And in case some of you out there are creeps: no, it is not acceptable to use this line and then call the woman yourself! You should never lie to a woman to get her phone number. Besides, you have no chance with this method. When she sees it's you, she's going to be so creeped out she's going to run and hide as fast as she can.

Of course, there's always the possibility she'll say she doesn't want to give your friend her number . . . she'd rather you have it. In which case, you can't really object, can you?

The Game Show Host

The Game Show Host is not a routine, it's an attitude. The key here is to have a game show host mentality—acting jolly, goofy, smiling, and selling everyone on the fact that they're having a good time. The goal is to get the woman (or women) laughing along with you, loosening up, and having a good time. Forget serious discussion and that work-school-hobby AFC conversation trap. Keep it simple, almost childish—and never forget to smile. High five your wing, suggest hand-holding and kissing between various parties, insist that everyone do body shots, demand a round of truth or dare, etc. The idea is that this bar is now your personal party, and you are going to make sure everyone hooks up. No one will think you're a creep, because you are hooking up everyone but yourself. Eventually, a girl (or your wing) will point out that *you* should do a body shot or a dare, as well. If the girls try to leave initially, insist that they stay, because while there may be a few awkward moments at the beginning, once you've gotten your act rolling they won't want to leave, even for a second.

The game show host approach is difficult, since the women need to be coaxed into your laid-back, silly world. It's best used with a group, so you can avoid the awkward silences of a woman who isn't really digging your act, and if everyone starts going along with it, she will too. Once you get going, feel free to turn and talk to strangers. Ignoring the girls for a minute is a reminder of how much fun they were having when you were paying attention to them, which will only make them try harder to keep your attention.

The Rich and Famous Setup

This one's a little suspect—I hate a dishonest approach—but I'm going to include it anyway. It can be a lot of fun, if only to prove once again that, incredibly, women are even more shallow than we are.

The Inadvertent Wing

Sometimes your wing isn't a friend or even a fellow PUA, he's just some hopeless AFC you don't even know, slobbering all over himself trying to score women to no avail. If you see some schmuck hitting on a girl and stalling, getting shot down and doing a crash and burn, don't pity or make fun of him in your mind when he walks away with his tail between his legs. Instead, use this perfect opportunity to leech from his miserable failure.

That girl is prime territory, so casually walk up to her and say, "I couldn't help but notice that encounter. That must have been one of the worst pick-up lines you've ever heard." She'll usually laugh or smile. Well, turn that smile into a heated conversation about terrible pick-up lines and loser AFCs. Show her that you understand, that you feel the same way. Suddenly, you have something in common, and it's bad pick-ups of all things! She will drop her shield because, in comparison to the last guy, you seem very sincere and interesting and . . . you're probably not trying to pick her up, right?

Yeah, right.

You're with your wingman and you see a woman across the room. Sure, you could both go game show host on her, but let's try something new. Instead of approaching, you have your wing move in on her and start chatting—without trying to pick her up. After a minute or two, have him call you over and introduce you. Say "hi," but look a little uncomfortable and leave soon after. "Poor guy," your wing says, "do not waste your time on him. Women hit on him all the time, but they're only after his money. He just gets so tired of it." She says, "Oh, he's rich?" "Unfortunately. And kind of famous, too." That's all. He has to keep it vague.

That's the setup. Now to put the plan into action, you approach her an hour later and ask if she's seen your trusty wingman. You'll know immediately if your plan has worked, because she'll start asking you leading questions, such as, "I could swear I thought I knew you earlier. Have we met before?" Remember to stay as vague and ambiguous as possible. Not only will this keep her from finding out the truth, it will make you seem mysterious and cagey, just like a famous person would be.

Give this fifteen minutes, then have your wing break into the conversation with a disapproving look . . . for her. Say you're glad to see him because you're bored and ready to go. She'll try to convince you to stay, but don't go for it, because if you insist on leaving (and thereby negging her), she is by this point almost guaranteed to offer you her phone number.

The Female Wing (a.k.a. "The Pivot")

A smooth wingman is one thing, but *nothing* attracts women to you faster than seeing you with another attractive woman on your arm. It's part jealously; part believing that if she sees something in you, then you must be the real deal. Plus, other women see you treating her with respect and attention, and they want to be treated that way, too. In PUA terms, this woman is a pivot; she first attracts all the attention herself, but then turns it toward the real attraction—you.

Pivots are women you like to spend time with, but for whatever reason you don't want to (or can't) have sex with them. They should be friends, not family, and the hotter they are, the better. They can be women who have told you they just want to be friends. Don't feel ashamed; go ahead and use that friendship. Or they can be co-workers, in case your work ethics forbid you to pursue possibilities more heated than a working relationship. Even better, pivots can be women that you previously picked up and slept with, but have now put into the LJBF zone. This woman may feel a bit jilted by being placed in the subordinate pivot role, but that's okay. Even if she tells the other woman behind your back that she slept with you and then you LJBF'd her . . . well, that only makes you more intriguing to the average female. You're clearly a hot and experienced lover—and they always think they can change you.

The most important thing is for pivots to understand their role and their place in your life. You are out to have a good time with each other, but they are not your date or partner (you don't want any thwarted expectations later). They have to understand that you will be approaching other women during the night, and go ahead and ask for their help. Pivots appreciate this honesty, and there is nothing better then having your pivot approaching the woman you want to score with, chat her up, then wave you over. That's like getting a recommendation from a member of the club!

And, yes, seeing you moving on all these other woman will often make a pivot hot and horny for your action herself. This is not the best way to turn on a reluctant chick, but it just might have that result—if you play it straight. Is there anything better than getting a woman's number, then going home and getting hot and heavy with your pivot? Only taking them both home at the same time, of course.

The Dynamics of Approaching a Group
(It's Easier Than You Think)

Approaching a group of females may seem like the ultimate in macho—after all, you're just throwing yourself to the vicious pack, right? Actually, no. Approaching a group of women, especially with a wingman, is not any harder than approaching one woman. In fact, it's probably even easier!

There are two general ways of approaching groups of people containing women who have caught your eye. The first one involves becoming the friend of the most bored people in the group; the second one requires you to become friends with more or less every member of the group. The first approach is easier for beginners, since your communication and socializing skills may not yet be up to the standards required to captivate the whole group at once. The downside, though, is you are less likely to end up with the girl you'd prefer and more likely to end up with the girl the group chooses for you or who is interested in you herself. The second approach, once mastered, is a lot more fun and, even more importantly, a lot more effective, since you'll be in control of awakening the interest and commanding the attention of the girl you want, plus make a lot of friends in the process.

Group Approach, Type 1: Get In, See Who Wants You

In this first approach, you're not trying to impress everybody. You only need to get okayed by one member first, then proceed to being okayed by the rest of the group, at which point you are free to proceed to the girl who seems to be showing the most interest in you.

Start by selecting the female member of the group who looks the most bored and start chatting with her. Do not try to pick her up. Just have a nice friendly conversation. Be fun and spontaneous. She may not be interested in you (she may be a sourpuss, a reason why she wasn't having any fun in the first place), but your presence will bring out the competitive juices in all the other women there. Soon enough, you'll be acquainted with other members of the group as well. And if one of the other women is interested in you, even slightly, she will let it be known by giving you eye contact or trying to join the conversation.

This is called self-selecting for you on the part of the group, and it's the real secret to why group dynamics are such a good way to meet women. And, of course, since you're a real PUA, there's no reason why you shouldn't give this process a little shove as well. In other words, why wait for the available girl to show herself, when you can easily draw her out?

As soon as you've been introduced around, and everyone's starting to feel comfortable, jump right into a leading question,

The Crappy Sketch Artist Approach

Here's a hilarious excuse for approaching a large group of women from that master of seduction, Ross Jeffries (www.seduction.com). This is the perfect way to target one female in the group and create initial eye contact with the object of your interest. You'll need a pen and a small-spiral bound notebook, because what you're going to do is furrow your brow, bend over your pad, and with utmost concentration sketch the target of your affection.

What's that you say? You can't even draw a smiley face without making it look constipated? Well, no problem because, in the words of guru Ross, "What you are actually doing on that pad of paper . . . is sketching the crappiest stick figure drawing of her that would embarrass a dyslexic five-year-old!"

Once you're done, and especially if the women have started to notice you and glance your way (which they usually do as you're kind of making a scene), sign it with a flourish and fold it in two. Now walk up to your subject and tell her, in the most humble of terms, that her beauty has inspired you to artistic ecstasy. Return to your seat and watch her open the page . . . and burst out laughing. Smile, wave, and take a little bow like you're proud of your work. About half the time, they will wave you over to the table and play along.

such as, "I'm curious. Which one of you has the most inquisitive and adventurous mind?" Almost always, the group will volunteer a girl. And you know who she'll be? The one they think you should be with! She may not be the most attractive girl in the group (and remember you can always eject later if she's a dog), but she's definitely going to be the one most in need of a man like you. So just make sure you have a good reason for asking who has a curious mind (e.g., I wanted to discuss an interesting problem with an intelligent woman), and you're in like Flynn.

Group Approach, Type 2:
Be a Friend, Disarm the Obstacles

The second group approach, more advanced but more effective, requires you not only to be okayed by everybody, but preferably to become friends with them, especially with the women (or men) whom we will identify as "obstacles."

Here's how it goes. You see a group of women. One of them is your target. The others, be they male or female, are obstacles. Poor sucker AFCs will make the same mistake every time and ignore the obstacles, trying to slobber their way into the target of their affection. That is a fatal flaw in their seduction plan.

An ignored obstacle is a dangerous obstacle. She (or he) is pissed by the dis, and will only get more pissed the longer the conversation continues. Remember, the target's friends have far more influence over her than you can hope to achieve in ten minutes of brilliant banter, which means that when they eventually start to interfere with your pick-up, dragging the target away, talking with her and ignoring you, making rude comments and breaking the mood, you're dead meat. If you're really good, the target may slip you her phone number on the fly as she's being dragged out of your life. More likely, though, the obstacle's poisonous tongue will have ruined your chances forever.

That's why suave PUAs always befriend the obstacles *before* the target. Being friends with her friends makes you look good, so spread yourself around, and have a good time doing it—shake hands, be humorous, give a few "I understand where you're coming from" nods. It's especially important to befriend the cranky, mouthy girl (who is usually the ugly one as well, not surprisingly) because she probably holds the moral strings on this crowd and isn't afraid to pull them at all the wrong times for you. Befriend her, play games with her, make her like you, and then, only then, turn your attention for the first time to the target.

Not only have you disarmed the obstacles, you've disarmed your target as well. Since your target is no doubt the most attractive female in the group, she is used to being the center of attention with men. But here you are, ignoring her, in front of

You approach an ugly girl and a hot babe standing together, talking. Which do you talk to first?

Always talk to the ugly girl first. The hot girl will be surprised, jealous, and intrigued. Now she's going to try that much harder to win you over. And the ugly girl is positively surprised as well. She's used to being ignored; therefore, you must be a really nice guy. In fact, she may decide you're a better match for her hot girlfriend—and you've just made an unexpected but insanely powerful ally! But even if she won't became an active ally, she most certainly won't become your active obstacle, which she would have become if you had ignored her in the first place.

everyone! This is bound to get her intrigued. She figures you're either accustomed to beautiful women (you're a stud), or you find something unattractive about her (and since she's used to being adored, she *must* find out what it is, immediately!). Either way, she's going to work that much harder to land you. Just keep acting like you're not that interested in her, talking to her as if you're doing her a favor, and she'll finally get so worked up she'll just have to have you.

Getting Separation (Wingman Version)

Once you've disarmed the obstacles and engaged the target, you need to get separation as soon as possible, and this is critical. Many girls—I would say a majority—are uncomfortable with their friends seeing them kissing or getting "friendly" with a stranger. They have their reputations to think about, and that jealous friend of hers could easily go running back to your target's mom or boyfriend, telling them what a slut their sweet little missy is. And how do you even know that "friend" she's with isn't her mother, niece, sister-in-law, co-worker, or even worse, her boss? In other words, as long as that friend is around, she has every reason not to take your bait—even if she wants to.

This is where your wingman comes in. It's his job to keep the friends distracted while you and the target melt away to a quiet corner. This works especially well when you're working on just two women, because as soon as you have struck up a rapport with your individual targets, you can just lean over to your girl and say that you think you should leave those two alone. Whisper this to her, because it's important that it look like you're making her a nasty proposition, and it's imperative that the friend has no idea what you're saying. Your girl probably questions your judgment (even if she's really into you she doesn't want to seem too eager with her friend there); just give her a slight push with something mildly insulting, like "Are you blind? Can't you see they want to be alone?" or "You don't want to watch them, do you? That's kind of odd for a first date."

Does it matter if your wing is about to get it on? Hell, no. The best part about this tactic is that it's a self-fulfilling prophecy. You've just put it in her mind that her friend is hot for your wing, so that makes you more attractive. Meanwhile, when you two leave, her friend can't help but think the two of you want to be alone so you can start in on the private fun. In other words, they both think the other one is going to be getting some in a few minutes—and neither wants to be left out of the fun. Voilà, two horny women eager to please!

Troubleshooting: But What About My Friends?

At some point, before she leaves with you, every self-respecting woman is going to stop and say, "Wait, I can't just leave my friends here." Don't fall for it. Don't even fall for the old "I need to tell my friends I'm leaving" line. This is a momentum killer, and it's very important that you keep the momentum moving forward. Just say something like, "Don't worry. They'll find their way home. We haven't seen them for ages, anyway, so they're clearly having a good time and not too worried about you." Then take her hand, lead her to the door, and jump in the nearest cab.

Getting Separation (Solo Version)

The best way to get a girl to leave the group is by having something you need to tell her in private. As soon as you get a break, just lean over and whisper to her, "Do you want to duck away for a second? I have something I know you'll enjoy more in private." Motion her away, preferably with a hand on the small of her back, and say to the others in the group, "Excuse us for a moment, I'll bring her right back." Once you've got her away from the hens, look around confidentially and say, "The reason I took you aside (pause) is because I wanted to tell you (long pause) your friends are nice and all but ... (don't tell her the secret until she either asks for it or really shows some interest) ... I just had to tell you that ..." Now give her a good, sincere compliment that has nothing to do with her beauty, such as telling her that she's a great conversationalist and you enjoy listening—you don't want to seem supplicating, after all—and follow up with, "I hope you're the kind of woman that can tell the difference between a pick-up (gesture away like that's clearly not your game) and a sincere compliment (give her a squeeze on the elbow or in some other way give her a touch to remember you by)." Now make some eye contact and walk away. After all, this is not the kind of invitation many women can refuse.

While this is a classic pick-up move, there is a variation that is a little bit riskier, but a lot of fun. When you see a beautiful woman in a group, approach her quietly, touch her lightly on the elbow, and ask very softly if you can speak with her for a minute. Then slowly walk away, but stop within clear sight (this is a good time to have a wing along so you don't look like a loner dork). The goal is to be so non-intrusive, so subtle, that you peak her curiosity without creeping her out. Even if she doesn't come over to you right away, there's a good chance that, if she sees you later in the evening, she'll just have to come over and say something to you.

If More Than One Woman Gives You the Vibe

When you're chatting up a group of beautiful women, it's usually pretty clear which one is into you and, therefore, which woman you should separate from the herd. Sometimes, however, you'll find yourself getting the vibe from more than one, usually two, but maybe even three women in the group. An embarrassment of riches! What's a lucky guy to do?

If there are two women giving you the vibe, extract them both. That's right, separate both women from the group together, even if one is better looking than the other. Yes, as long as they're both lovable, extract them both. If you don't, you're just going to anger the one you rejected and turn her into a major obstacle. Instead, pull them both aside (if they're really giving you the vibe this should be easy) and start your own little two (or three)-on-one conversation. Don't play favorites, but play along with their games. If you're lucky, the two of them will start to try to outdo each other with turning you on.

If one of them decides to go back to the group, let her go. This will almost always be the end result, and it's perfect because you have essentially let them choose between themselves which one gets you. In other words, you end up with the eager one, and nobody gets their feelings hurt.

But even if both of them try to return to the group, don't worry. Just say, "Now, I *know* one of you wants to stay with me," and that will usually get the more eager one to pull back to you.

In other words, if two girls are giving you the business, don't choose because you may lose.

And yes, it's possible to extract *and* go home with both women, but don't count on it. If you try to suggest an orgy (except as a GM-style joke), you're just going to lose them both 99 percent of the time. Nice try, though, Romeo—the effort deserves applause, and the one success *more* than makes up for ninety-nine failures.

CHAPTER **7**

Dancing

The Do's and Don'ts of Dancing

"A woman I know and trust advised me one time that, in her humble opinion, if a man can't dance, he probably can't fuck either. . . . Being able to dance well demonstrates that you are comfortable in your body and know how to use it with precision and control."

—Jake Thomson, ASF

Throughout history, dancing has been a pre-copulation ritual and a primary criterion for choosing a mate. If you're good, then dancing is a great way to attract women. Just slip in with the most beautiful women, and you'll get their attention plus the attention of everyone else on and off the floor.

But let's face it: most of us aren't great dancers. That's one of the primary reasons a dance club is not a great place to meet women (they're also expensive and often too loud for intimate conversation). One possibility, then, is to put a lot of time and effort into becoming a good dancer. I'm not saying this is a bad idea and it probably will help you with your horizontal moves between the sheets—but it's not necessary.

Always keep in mind, though, that dancing with a woman is not your ultimate goal. It is, at best, a tool to move you closer to your real goals—getting close enough to kiss, feeling her up and tonguing her down, making her cum right there in the club, making her cum later back at your place, or even better, all of the above. The real magic of the dance is not in sweeping her off her feet, but in using those old PUA tools that come in handy in any situation—a smile, eye-contact, and some well-timed kino.

In other words, do your dance, have fun, then get your woman off the dance floor and into a quiet, private place where you can lay it on her and make the sparks fly.

The exception to this rule are the so called "kino girls." They love being touched, and they love touching you in return. Should you encounter a girl like that (and believe me, you'll know it immediately), don't leave the dance floor. Just keep rubbing, touching, kissing, and grinding. Once the touching gets intimate, it's straight off the dance floor and into your car. This kind of girl hates talking, so don't waste your time. Chances are, while you're laying down your lines, she'll just be getting frustrated and wondering why you aren't touching her. Frustrating a woman by not reading her right is classic AFC.

Initiating Contact

If you're at a dance club, it's important to get on the dance floor. Standing on the sidelines is for wallflowers. When there's a line of men ringing the dance floor, that's called "death row." That's right, those guys are already doomed, and I bet you don't want all the gorgeous women in the club to associate you with those corpses. Remember, your goal is to lure women off the dance floor and into your quiet corner, and in order to do that, you actually have to step onto the dance floor yourself.

The best way to get a girl dancing with you isn't by talking with her, it's by initiating contact. Dancing is a purely physical activity, so use the environment and *touch* that woman. And the best place to do that isn't from the sidelines, it's from the dance floor.

But She's Already Dancing With . . .

It's pretty easy to cut in on a dance in the heat of the dance floor, but it's not always easy to stay with the girl you want. Vilius (ASF) offers a solution to breaking up a couple (even if a friend is the male) and staying with the woman:

> Interrupt them by taking over the *male* partner and just start dancing with him. . . . After some thirty seconds you can turn around, grab the girl, gently pull her a few feet away and continue dancing with her.

That's a fairly good tip, except for a couple of minor problems. First, don't ever cut in on a friend, unless it's clear that he is striking out. That is just uncool. Second, thirty seconds is an awfully long time. You're better off judging the reaction of the woman and playing it by instinct. If she wasn't into the guy in the first place, or didn't know him from a hole in the wall, then she may turn away almost immediately. In that case, you better react immediately too, because not only is she now free, she owes you one for rescuing her from that spastic chump.

Remember, this rule also applies to two women dancing together. Start dancing with the ugly one first, and turn to your target only after you've got her friend nice and impressed. It's called disarming the obstacles, remember?

If your primary target is already dancing, just maneuver into position and start dancing with her. You'll know soon enough whether she's taken your bait. This works even better with a group of women. They are usually totally receptive to having a guy wiggle his way into their midst, and you'll usually get one of the women to pick you out for some dirty dancing. Whether she'll want to leave the dance floor with you is another question (she's with her friends, so she's got her reputation to think

Chump File: Asking for a Dance

Of course, you could just walk up to a girl and say, "Would you like to dance with me?" After all, it's always a good idea to be supplicating and whiny, giving the woman all the power and the perfect opportunity to reject you before even getting to know you.

This is a classic AFC strategy: cutting off your options and putting yourself at the mercy of the woman. When you *ask* her to dance, if she says yes, great! If she says no, you're screwed. You can try and salvage the situation by engaging her in conversation, but you started with her rejecting you, so now your job is significantly harder.

Of course, you could always just move on to another girl, but unfortunately she just saw you get rejected. Who do you think she is, some low-standard hussy that picks up on the scraps that other women throw aside? You're just setting yourself up for that most humiliating of experiences: moving from girl to girl, and being turned down by all of them, until you run out of girls to ask. Okay, that's unlikely. Someone will eventually dance with you, but it will probably be (yep, you guessed it) the least attractive girl in the place. She's the only one desperate enough to dance with the AFC, even with the stink of rejection all over him.

The worst part is, the rejection isn't necessarily personal. Why? Because by being a supplicating AFC, you let a number of factors out of your control come into play. What if she's tired? Waiting for a friend in a designated spot? Has a boyfriend around the corner? Or just doesn't dance, ever (in which case she probably doesn't fuck either, so who cares)? If you supplicate, you're just encouraging her to make excuses. If you're direct and forceful, closing off her ability to say no, then all these concerns will go out the window as will that AFC boyfriend stupid enough to leave a beautiful woman standing by the dance floor all alone.

Of course, even if you ask and get turned down, you can still save the situation by having the next woman take you up on your offer. Remember, there is nothing more of a turn-on to women then seeing that other women are hot for your action. So whatever you do, don't compound your error by standing there and arguing with her about why she won't dance with you. There's always a better-looking and cooler girl standing right behind her, and you're what she's been waiting for her whole life.

Just don't make the same mistake and *ask* her to dance, too.

---

about), but her body language will tell you how intimate she wants to get. Besides, if she's into you, she can always slip away from her friends later, so keep your eye on that prize.

Your other option is to dance near the edge of the floor and pull a passing girl onto the floor with you. If you prefer to use this strategy without the wiggle (which is definitely recommended if you're a bad dancer), then use this method:

Approach your target from between her and the dance floor. With a big smile, take her hand (the most important step), nod toward the floor, and say, "Come on!" If she seems reluctant, give her a gentle pull toward the floor (and you), and say, "Well, come on!" If she makes an excuse (such as "I'm tired") then, boom, you're in conversation. "Tired? Well this place is a little crowded and noisy. Why don't we sit down someplace quiet and just relax for a minute?" You're, of course, still holding her hand, but now you're guiding her away from the floor toward the nice little corner you scoped out beforehand.

Save Your Dignity

You asked a girl to dance (in spite of what I told you) and guess what, she said "no." Well, your only option now is a snappy comeback and hitting the road. The following lines won't actually make her want you, but since she's a lost cause anyway (and it took about two seconds to come to this, all because of a simple mistake), then what the heck? At least you can cheer yourself up a bit at her expense.

Option 1

You: Do you want to dance?

Her: No.

You: *(looking confused)*: Oh, no, no, no. I said you look fat in those pants.

Option 2

You: Do you want to dance?

Her: No.

You: Oh, come on! Lower your standards. I did.

Slow Dancing

Slow dancing is the next best thing to public fornication, and it's the reason you let your wingman talk you into coming out to this nightclub in the first place. As soon as you hear a slow dance starting up, you must make your move. Take the girl you're currently talking with to the dance floor—unless you're already in a very intimate moment, of course. If you're in that three second period between leaving one girl and hooking up with another (you haven't just been standing around, looking at the hot bodies, but unable to approach, have you?), either return immediately to the girl you just left (if you're close to her) or scoop up the first available target in your immediate vicinity.

The key to slow dancing is to be bold, yet sensitive and attentive. Be bold—hold her close to your body, start rubbing her back with your hand. Be sensitive—watch for her reactions and jump on any opportunity. If she isn't reacting positively, just keep working closer to her slowly, feeling her out, giving her every opportunity to respond. It might just be that she's shy and needs a little warming up. If not, then thank her for the dance at the end of the song and suggest you go someplace more quiet for a chat. Don't forget to keep holding her hand!

If she starts to rub your shoulders, chest, or neck, move in and put your body against hers. If she starts to grind against you, grind back and start kissing her neck. Work your way up behind the ear, then the earlobe, then the cheek, then the lips. At this point, you can forget about talking—this is a kino girl. You should either stay on the floor, kissing and grinding slowly and deliciously, even if a fast song comes on, or you should take her to a dark corner for some more private heavy petting. Eventually, you're going to want to call a cab or, even better, check and see if the coatroom of the club is available.

After the Dance

It goes without saying that you won't end the dance with a "thanks, see you around" while you walk away. You didn't come here to wiggle it just a little bit. So don't let her do the same.

After the dance ends, take her hand and lead her off the dance floor to the quiet corner of your choice, *even if she wants to keep dancing* (unless she's a "kino girl," of course). Don't let go of that hand. If it seems like she is about to bail, just lean over and whisper in her ear something along the lines of, "I want to tell you something." She'll probably ask, "About what?" Just reply, "I'll tell you when we sit down."

Fast Dance to Slow Dance

You've seen them before: a guy and girl on the dance floor, ignoring all the other people diligently wiggling to the fast pace of the music and having a slow dance all their own, touching, kissing. A newly married couple on a honeymoon? Think again, because that guy in there could and should have been you.

Here's a classic fast-dance-to-slow-dance move, as observed by Maniac High. The key to this technique is patience. The PUA doesn't rush the woman. He makes sure she's ready for the next step *before* making it—and he doesn't do anything sexual, nothing at all, until she's wet and about to literally burst open with anticipation.

The scene is the standard one you've seen a thousand times. A dance floor full of people, flashing lights, the same fast-paced dance mix played all the time at every club in the world.

1. Begin dancing, facing the woman. Try to mirror her moves, and always keep eye contact with her. (duration: approximately 3 minutes)
2. Start the kino by putting your arm on her side. Slowly, with a light touch, move your arm to her back. Keep pace with the music and maintain eye contact. Once you have the first arm on her back, do the same thing with your second arm, but don't pull her towards you yet. (duration: approximately 2 minutes)
3. Slowly rub your hands up her back, and use light pressure to cause her to raise up her arms (you aren't coercing her, remember). Rub all the way up her arms, then rub slowly down to her ass. Let your hands rest on her hips. Don't grope her (yet). While doing this move, subtly slow down your pace. The woman will slow

down, mimicking you, and may not even notice that you are no longer following the music. (duration: approximately 4 minutes)

4. With your hands on her hips, slowly tilt in your head and lightly breathe on her neck. Don't try to kiss her yet.

5. Move your hands up and down her back slowly. As you do, move your head around her neck, breathing slowly. Keep your head close. Keep your eyes open and watch her. She may close her eyes now, feeling the sexual contact. (duration: approximately 3 minutes)

6. Move your head and hands down her body, staying close to her as you move down. Let your hands go all the way down to her knees, then back up, always keeping your body crouched close to hers. She should be writhing slowly at the contact. Your head will go as low as her stomach. Try *not* to pay any special attention to her tits—you're turning her on but not doing anything overtly sexual. After moving back up, breathe on her neck again. (duration: approximately 3 minutes)

7. Move your hands up her back, again coaxing her to raise her arms. This time, though, when you move back down, pull her close to your body. Her eyes should be closed, but don't close yours unless she looks directly at you. If you've moved correctly, she should be deep into the trance. (duration: approximately 3 minutes)

8. Again, rub your hands to the top of her arms, but this time, break contact at the top and leave your hands in the air. Stay close to her. She should take the hint and begin the rubbing routine on you. (duration: approximately 4 minutes)

9. Turn her around so that her back is to your front. This is an awkward moment—it breaks contact and puts her out of her trance state—lean in and blow gently on her

neck, then whisper something ("I love to watch you dance") in her ear. Remember, you haven't exchanged a single word yet, so just the sound of your voice is a powerful intoxicant.

10. Follow the same routine (hands in the air, down to the knees), but do not touch her tits or crotch. The anticipation is building. (duration: approximately 4 minutes)

11. Turn her around again and pull her close against you, breathing on her neck. She should breathe on you as well. At this point, she should be leaning on you, anticipating more, but you keep the anticipation building. You'll be dancing very slowly and close together, despite the throbbing music. Don't rush anything. (duration: approximately 5 minutes)

12. Move up to her face, getting just inches away from her lips but don't kiss her. She won't know whether you're waiting for her or just making her sick with anticipation. It doesn't matter—she's practically begging for your touch at this point. (Spend 4 minutes—that's right, 4 minutes—of your lips being only a millimeter from hers, your breath mingling.)

13. The kiss begins and it goes on and on and on.

Is there a better way to spend thirty-five minutes on the dance floor? I don't think so. And that's not even including the kiss!

Basically, you're using the same strategy you would use to separate a woman form a group. In this case, though, the "group" is the music and the dance floor.

PART

3

The Conversation

CHAPTER **8**

Speed Seduction®

Speed Seduction®

*"I give men a massive and quick way to decide on
a woman's potential and to create an attraction.
This is not about dating. Speed Seduction® is
meant to replace dating. Dating is for women
you're already sleeping with."*

—Ross Jeffries, legendary PUA and creator
of Speed Seduction®

Speed Seduction® is—let's go ahead and say it—the revolution-
ary approach to picking up women created and promoted by
Ross Jeffries (www.seduction.com), perhaps the most important
man in the field of seduction science since Casanova. Jeffries'
technique relies on using patterns of pre-set conversations to
create certain expectations and feelings in a woman's mind.
Understanding the essence of Ross Jeffries' Speed Seduction® is
useful because it reveals, in simple terms, the most important
aspect of having a "conversation" with a beautiful woman.
Namely, that everything you say and do must lead her to the
place you want her to be—turned on and totally into you.

Speed Seduction® grew out of the work of John Grinder and Richard Bandler, who studied and taught at the University of California, Santa Cruz in the early 1970s. The professors theorized that any subjective human experience—from something terrible to something wonderful (like love)—could easily be transformed in the mind through the subtle use of hypnotic language patterns, embedded commands, and other vocal tricks. The two doctors began to use the technique in psychoanalysis, using language to put their subjects into a light trance and then "curing" them of their traumas. They called the practice neurolinguistic programming (NLP), and despite skepticism from the professional community, it worked!

And that's where Ross Jeffries comes in. In his day job, Jeffries uses NLP to help cure men of shyness and phobias. But then he had a brainstorm. If this technique can cure men, he thought, why wouldn't it seduce women? Guess what? It did.

Ross Jeffries had stumbled onto an important secret: it's the words you use and the actions you perform that create expectations in a woman. The goal in seduction is not to talk to a woman, but to *guide* her to a state of excitement. Ross Jeffries does this using pre-programmed patterns; in this guide, you'll learn to do it by genuinely listening to and understanding the expectations and desires of the woman you're talking to.

In both listening to and understanding the woman, the underlying goal is getting the woman to want to become intimate with you. Always keep that goal in mind while striving towards the moment when you can kiss her or take her home for the night.

So, before we move on to a general discussion of seductive conversation, let's dig a little bit deeper into Speed Seduction®. Remember, though, this is only a general discussion, an outline if you will. If you want more detailed information on speed seduction®, visit Ross Jeffries's website at www.seduction.com.

Patterning

Patterns form the core of Ross Jeffries' Speed Seduction® technique. Patterns are scripts intended to create a certain state of anticipation, excitement, and connection in the targeted woman. The patterns are generally stories that describe various wonderful states of mind and feelings that seemingly have nothing to do with you and her (music, dancing, riding a roller coaster, and eating strawberries and chocolate), but which, unconsciously, get her aroused. It goes without saying that, since you're the man who got her aroused and made her feel wonderful things she had long forgotten or never even experienced, and since you did all that with your words alone, she probably doesn't even dare to imagine what you could do with your . . . nah, she's imagining it already.

Describing the feeling of excitement, though, isn't enough. Patterning also uses embedded commands that will focus her mind and attention on what you're saying. This involves saying things in the context of a story. For example, you could describe the anticipation you felt on cresting the hill of a large roller coaster: "Feel the excitement building . . . focus on those feelings . . . surrender completely . . ." She may even be aroused by these subtle alpha male commands, but at the very least she will become more attentive to what you're saying and what you have to offer.

Patterns also contain subconscious messages known as binder commands. For example, they may say, " . . . that's the way to do it. Now, with me, it's different because . . ." What the woman hears, both unconsciously and as a result of your subtle inflection, is "Do it! Now! With me!" This serves to bind all her feelings of desire and arousal to you.

The final aspect of patterning is sexual suggestion. Your words may sound innocent in context, but she is bound to pick up on their more naughty innuendoes unconsciously. Once you have her imagining all these phrases out of context, don't be surprised if she says she has to go to the bathroom, and her seat is all wet. A few examples of these sexually suggestive phrases are: "Create an opening for it . . . feel that thought penetrate you . . . you come over and over again to the same conclusion . . ." I think you see what I mean.

Even more devious and subtle are the so-called weasel phrases, which use double-meaning pronunciations to give her direct sexual suggestions and commands. Now, these will sound really funny the first time you hear them explained, and the jury is still out on their actual effectiveness, but there are those who swear by them so I'll give a few examples. For instance, in the weasel-phrase world, the phrase "these values are below me" is pronounced "blow me"; "a feeling of happiness" becomes "happenis"; "thoughts flowing in a new direction" becomes "nude erection"; and instead of saying "the sky is so beautiful" (how innocent is that!) you're really saying "this guy is so beautiful" (meaning yourself, of course). Said in context, but pronounced out of context, these phrases will supposedly have the woman unconsciously imagining the double meaning without being able to consciously object. Since it's a fact you were talking about a "new direction," not a "nude erection," she'd look like a moron to try to call you on your come-on or contradict your statement. She'll just have to keep quiet and keep her naughty images to herself.

Of course, the main value of the patterns is their ability to make a girl recall or imagine absolutely wonderful feelings and unconsciously link them to you. The other important value is that, at least at the start, you don't have to come up with your own conversation. In fact, you don't really have to interact with the woman at all. You can just lay down a few conversational patterns that have already been tried and tested by countless gurus of seduction, and that really takes the pressure off.

Although canned patterns are only a stepping-stone to the higher art of being able to pattern on the fly, the existing ones work perfectly when used in context in a conversation. Just make sure they sound natural, *not* like something you've rehearsed in advance to pick up chicks. After all, only a pervert would do something like that, right?

The "Discovery Channel" Pattern, Courtesy of Ross Jeffries (www.seduction.com)

This pattern is from the master of Speed Seduction® himself, Ross Jeffries. This pattern is his most famous, and one of his most effective. Some people say—though I've never had this happen myself—that using this pattern can make a woman cum. As I said, I'm not sure if this is true, and I'd much rather be participating physically if she did. At any rate, I definitely recommend this pattern.

You: You know, I saw the most interesting show on the Discovery Channel last night. They were interviewing people who make their living designing attractions for amusement parks like Magic Mountain and Disneyland and Universal Studios. Wouldn't that be a cool way to make a living?

Her: Yeah! That sounds so interesting.

You: Well, anyway, they were talking about the elements that make up the ideal attraction. They said there are three parts to the ideal attraction. First, when you EXPERIENCE the ideal attraction, you FEEL A STATE OF HIGH AROUSAL. The ideal attraction makes your heart beat faster, and your breathing gets faster and you just FEEL THAT AMAZING RUSH all over.

Her: Yeah!

You: And then they said that another part to an ideal attraction is that its fascinating. You just FEEL SO ENTHRALLED that you want to TAKE THIS RIDE (*subtle point to your pecker!*) multiple times; as soon as you GET OFF you want to GET BACK ON again.

Her: Yeah!

You: And they said, finally, the most important element, is a sense of overall safety. That even though the attraction may look a little dangerous, you're CERTAIN YOU'RE SAFE. You

FEEL SAFE because you realize nothing bad can really happen, so that allows you to FEEL TOTALLY FREE to LET GO AND ENJOY THAT GREAT AROUSAL again and again and again. Can you (*squeeze her hand*) feel that is pretty close to the way it is?

Her: Oooh . . . yeah!!

You: When you imagine how much fun it is to ride a roller coaster or any other kind of amusement park ride . . . it's like, as that ride is climbing up and up, you can feel your heart pounding with excitement; you feel that you're breathing faster and faster, sometimes you're even gasping and panting, you feel the blood rushing through every part of your body and, as that excitement and tension is building and building, you reach the top of the ride and then as it crests, you just release it in a flood of excitement, and sometimes you're screaming you're so turned on.

And you know, afterwards I thought to myself, isn't that the totally accurate description of your ideal attraction to another person. You know that kind of wonderful click right in the center of who you are that just makes you feel totally drawn to this person and, on one hand, makes you feel totally safe and totally comfortable, like you were meant to know them and, at the same time, as if you've known them forever.

Stacking Realities

An important element of Speed Seduction® is redirecting your commands and suggestions. In other words, you are essentially dictating to her the feelings you want her to feel, but you are acting as if they are coming from somewhere else: your own feelings, a hypothetical situation, a friend, a television show, or magazine. This is called stacking realities.

On the simplest level, this is just a simple case of framing your command. "Have you ever felt that wonderful feeling of . . ." isn't really a question, it's a suggestion for her to feel that

If She's Working (a Short but Sweet Little Pattern)

You: You must get awful tired by the end of the day/night.

Her: (*She nods.*)

You: Do you ever get a chance to go on vacation?

Her: (*She says something.*)

You: What's your favorite type of vacation spot, I mean like your ideal (*self-point*), dream place to be (*subtle crotch motion*)?

Her: (*She describes somewhere, to which, of course, you play along until . . .*)

You: I'll tell you what else is great. That feeling when you get home after a hard day of work and all you can think about is stripping off your clothes and sliding into a hot bath or taking a shower.

Her: (*She says something.*)

You: You know how sometimes, before you even get into the bath water, you imagine the heat just working its way through every part of your body, making you feel so wonderful and relaxed, and then you actually slide in, just kind of ease into the wetness, and that warmth just takes you and you surrender to it?

Her: (*She speaks briefly.*)

You: It's too bad there are all these distractions and interruptions here. Do you want to meet me after work?

---

wonderful feeling right now. There's the reality of what you're saying, and then there's the other layer: the reality you want to create. The secret is to stack them together and make them one and the same.

Patterning also relies heavily on quoting, in which you say something as if it came from someone else, or as if it's merely something you observed. Here's an example from Ross Jeffries (www.seduction.com):

> Some men are so crude. I can't believe what I saw this dude do the other night. He walked up to this girl sitting at the bar next to me and said to her, "Imagine us totally making out and you getting so incredibly turned on by it. If you were to feel that right now, try not to think about having me eat your pussy all night long and getting really horny." I can't believe a guy would ask a woman to think about that all night long.

Or, this slight variation as an opener:

> You know I often ask women what they think is the worst pick-up line they ever heard. What's yours? [She responds.] Yeah, that's pretty bad, but you wouldn't believe the one this woman told me about. This guy walked up to her in a bar, looked her right in the eye (*take her hand and look her right in the eye*) and said, "Imagine me going down on you just the way you like it all night long and you were getting so hot and so wet that you were begging to have me inside you." Did that jerk really expect her to have those thoughts? With me, I would never say such a thing.

Of course, what you've done is asked her to think about making out with you and having you eat her pussy all night long, but you've presented it in such a way that the words—and anything potentially negative associated with them—don't come directly from you.

Quoting is a great tool because it creates distance between you and a subject. This is very important with more timid or insecure girls, who may not feel at ease with your delivery. If neither of you are overtly involved in the anecdote, she'll be much more receptive to thinking about what you're saying— and getting her thinking about you and her and sex is the whole basis of Speed Seduction®.

Quoting is particularly useful when you're jumping ahead to sex talk, as in the above example. Sex talk is essential to seduction, but very dangerous; with quoting, you've planted the idea in her mind, while remaining immune to any negative feelings (and negative reactions, like a quick slap to the face).

On the other hand, quoting can be a hindrance when you're dealing with open-minded and adventurous girls. These women want you to address their feelings directly and to talk about your own feelings, both lusty and otherwise. Quoting just makes you seem wimpy, and in this case creates a distance between you where there doesn't need to be one. If she's receptive, move right in for the kill and make that personal connection.

Delivering Patterns

Memorizing patterns alone won't win the woman of your dreams; you have to use them in the correct way, with the right attitude and delivery. Here are a few guidelines that are key to seducing women, with or without patterns. Remember these rules because, no matter your approach, they'll come in handy.

Watch your intonation. To be effective, a pattern needs to sound natural, but you also need to sell her on the important parts. Try to emphasize the embedded commands and suggestions, and always make it clear that your conversation is sincere. If you're talking about how wonderful an experience feels, really get into it and make your voice sound like that wonderful feeling.

Use body language. Back up your words, and especially the subconscious suggestions, with appropriate actions. The most effective of these is the self-point. Whenever you say something is wonderful or make a sexual suggestion, subtly motion with your hand toward yourself (or even toward your crotch for a sexual suggestion), binding that wonderful feeling to you. It also works in reverse. If you make a suggestion about something being penetrated or wet, subtly motion toward the woman.

Be Vague. Being vague lets her link the feelings you describe to her own personal experiences or dreams. It also keeps you romantic, thrilling, and mysterious—exactly the man you want to be.

Combine feeling with body sensations. You've got her thinking about how good something makes her feel; now hit her immediately with something that makes her feel a great physical sensation—wind in her hair, ice on her skin on a hot day. As Ross Jeffries (www.seduction.com) says, "The effect is practically irresistible, and the power isn't additive . . . it's exponential!"

Observe her responses. If you're worried about yourself—am I doing it right, how do I look, does she like me, she's coming around but what if I blow it now and never get laid—you will never get laid. With that kind of attitude, you *will* blow it. Remember, the most important person in the seduction situation is the woman. You have to understand how she's feeling and respond appropriately. This is vitally important, so we'll talk about it much more later.

Be flexible yet persistent. If a pattern isn't working, you don't give up. Just move on to the next one and keep doing that until you get a hit. Your transition to a different pattern doesn't even have to make sense. You can simply throw in something like, "Here's another thing," or "Here's something else that's interesting," and keep going. The important thing is not to let the woman throw you just because her guard is up. Her guard is there for a reason: to keep the weak, sniveling, quitters away. Show her that you are not that sniveling quitter.

Learn to love your mistakes. I've said it once, but let me say it again: "failure" to pick up a woman isn't a negative. It's simply a learning experience. As a PUA, you never attach too much meaning to any one woman. You know there's always someone better around the corner—and now that you've learned what doesn't work, you're that much closer to being successful. Never get discouraged because a woman was foolish enough to turn you down. As Ross Jeffries says, "If all you learn to do is really

---

Behind the Curve

You're chatting away about feelings, experiences, wonderful encounters and the woman doesn't seem to be responding. It's possible she's blowing you off. But it's also possible that she hasn't really had any of these wonderful experiences and she's having a hard time keeping up. Just slow down, really explain these wonderful feelings, and give her time to absorb everything. Sometimes it really takes a while—a few hours, days, or even a month—but when she comes around, she'll be ready to bang you. And yes, this really does happen.

---

begin to live the attitude that there are no failures, only learnings, you will be ahead of 99 percent of the people in society."

Thought Binding

"Every decision people make is based in and dependent on their state of mind. If you don't like their decision, change their state of mind."

—Ross Jeffries (www.seduction.com)

In Speed Seduction®, you would never approach a woman and tell her how wonderful, caring, and handsome you are. Instead, you would approach a woman and start to talk about how wonderful it is to meet someone that makes you feel special and wonderful. In other words, you're still trying to impress her with what a great guy you are, but now you're coming at it from a different angle. Instead of trying to bust through the (locked) front door, you're sneaking in the back.

Is she ready to have her back door violated like that? Well, there's no need to leave that kind of thing to chance, when you could subtly guide her in that direction without her even knowing she's been led.

This is called Thought Binding, and the idea is to use subtle commands to open up her mind to new experiences. You are telling her mind what direction to move in, and because her mind is not used to these kinds of commands (and therefore not used to rejecting them), it obeys. Here's an example from Ross Jeffries on binding her thoughts early on in the encounter:

> Hey, did you ever meet someone and just instantly know that you had to get to know this person better *(point to yourself)*? Maybe you felt something inside and got all excited about how much fun it'd be to get to know him and how curious and intrigued you'd feel? As you remember those feelings while we're talking, I'm just curious, do you first imagine how much fun they'd be to hang out with, and then get intrigued, or do you get intrigued first and then imagine how much fun this *(point to yourself)* would be?

What's happened? In essence, you're creating a receptive frame of mind by:

1. Having her recall the mood you want her in (the thought direction), and then
2. Giving her a command to stay in that mood while she talks to you (binding the thought to the present situation)

Thought Binding is not only a command; it's a presupposition. There's no guarantee you're going to have a conversation, but you've placed that thought in her mind. Then you've told her she's going to remember that thought (instead of asking her if she'll try to remember, for instance). And you know what? It works! She will stay in the mood throughout the conversation, and she'll find you mesmerizing, fascinating, and irresistibly attractive, without knowing why.

At least that is the teaching of Ross Jeffries. Is it true? Thousands have testified that it is. But for our purposes, there's a larger concept here. You've got to believe in that positive future from the moment you step up and start talking to her, and you've got to make her believe in it, too. If you're not pre-supposing a positive outcome and if you're not really believing and focusing all your energy on getting there, then all your efforts will prove futile.

Common Misconceptions About Patterning

Patterning is a powerful tool, but it's often misunderstood. Let's address some common misconceptions about patterning, before they begin to worry us. And, as always, this advice can be applied to any seduction.

Misunderstanding #1: Patterns Are Manipulative and Offensive to Women

Seducing women is not offensive; it is a compliment. You are actually giving women a wonderful gift. She has an affliction: it's called boredom, the ho-hums, the dread of hearing the same thing and having the same experiences every day. You have the cure: the ability to make her experience feelings and desires that she can't get every day. Why would you deny her that pleasure?

This misconception often manifests itself in the fear of "getting caught" running a pattern, as if trying to seduce a beautiful woman is a crime. If the woman discovers you're laying down some memorized lines on her, the truth is that she probably will walk away—but not because what you're doing is wrong. She'll walk away because she thinks you're a loser who can't think of something original to say. But remember, you're not doing anything wrong; you're just doing it the wrong way.

Misunderstanding #2: Patterns Are a Way to Sell Faulty Merchandise

Some people assume that if you're using patterns (or they're using patterns), it's because you can't pick up the woman with your looks, personality, or wallet. Puh-lease. If you entertain that attitude even for one minute, you are nothing more than a pathetic AFC. Is seduction some sort of trick? Is it a sign of weakness to actually be good at something? Or is it a sign of strength? I think you know the answer to that question.

Understand this: patterns are not a way of making up for what you lack. They are a way of giving the woman what *she* lacks, and what she truly wants: a deep, emotional, and imaginative experience with a powerful man.

Misunderstanding #3: Patterns Are Like Begging for Goodies

No, sir. Patterns aren't about securing a gift for you; they are about *giving* a gift to her. You are creating such incredible states of pleasure in her that eventually she will want to give you her goodies. In fact, she will be so hot for it she will practically have to give them to you. When you approach a woman, you're giving her something she didn't have before: excitement. That woman is about to receive an incredible gift from you, a gift she might continue to receive if she's smart, hot, and adventurous enough to keep you coming back for more. If she can't handle it, then you'll just give it to someone else. That's called confidence, and you better have it or you'll be thrown back in the AFC pool with the rest of the losers. Obviously, that is not what you want, so be a real man and change your attitude. You're using patterns to give a gift, not secure one.

Misunderstanding #4: Patterns Are Talking at a Girl, Not with Her

Patterns aren't just about laying down a shtick. Sure, some girls will sit quietly, getting dreamy and wet, just thinking about what you're saying. In a vast majority of cases, however, the pattern is just a lead into conversation. When a woman is really turned on, she will answer back to you, relating her personal feelings and important experiences—and maybe even her secret kinks and fantasies. What do you do? You listen, of course, and then tailor your patterns to her responses. Speedboats really rev her motor? Pattern them in. Daddy's girl? You can give her that wonderful feeling she had in those summers long ago just walking in the sunshine with her father. Hell, she can even sit on your lap!

Misunderstanding #5: Patterns Are Guaranteed Coochie, So If I Fail to Bag My Babe Using Patterns I Must Be a Real Loser

Wrong again, maestro. In fact, even for the real experts, patterns only work about 70 percent of the time. But imagine that— seven out of every ten women you approach will want to sleep with you! What about the rest of them? Well, those women are fools who are missing out on the best experiences of their lives. In this case, patterning hasn't failed you; it's helped you by keeping you away from the stiffs and the lamebrains.

Misunderstanding #6: Patterns Are Just for Horndogs

No way, José. Patterns are a way of life; a different way of looking at the world. If you embrace patterns (and the seduction mind-set), you become the person you've always wanted to be. You're confident, because you know you can control any conversation or situation. You're dominant, because you exert that control. You're fun to be around, because you always focus on what others are thinking and feeling, and then you use that knowledge to lead them to new heights of pleasure. Yes, even ugly women, other men, your boss, and, gulp, your parents. You're not trying to seduce these people, of course, but you can use the concept of guiding a conversation to elicit and fulfill their desires. You have the power—so get out there and use it!

Advanced Patterning

This has been just a brief introduction to the world of Speed Seduction®. It is an overview of the philosophy and general guidelines for becoming a patterning guru. It is by no means a comprehensive course. For that, you will need to contact the man himself, Ross Jeffries, at www.seduction.com.

In fact, just learning a few patterns has very little to do with Speed Seduction®. Running patterns on women is just the start of Ross Jeffries' philosophy. The real goal is to be able to use the patterns as examples, as a way to launch yourself into a conversation with a woman that is a mutual exploration of how you really think and feel about certain topics. Once you're adept at patterning, all conversations naturally fall into a pattern-like language, a confident language that throbs with power and sexual desire. As you pick up on her likes, desires, and kinks, throw them back at her by using her trance words and personal phrases, reinforcing the connection. It's no longer a "mind-fuck," as some crude beginners and outsiders mistakenly imagine it to be—it's a consensual probing of all the wonderful places the two of you have been and would like to go in the future.

In this way, it's exactly like the seduction techniques I'm going to teach you in the upcoming chapter: it's a way to make a sincere connection, to create sexual tension, and to suggest ways to relieve that hot, burning desire (and, yes, right about here is where you would self-point).

CHAPTER **9**

The Basic Rules of Engagement

Demonstrate Value and Personality

What is the goal of a conversation with a beautiful woman? What makes her want to take the time to talk with you and give you her number? No, it's not looks. It's the fact that you've demonstrated value and personality.

You have nothing, absolutely nothing to expect from a girl to whom you do not demonstrate value and personality. You have to show her something of value, something that makes her like the way she feels when she's around you. This is the entire basis of seduction, so I'm going to say it again: your goal is to make the woman *like the way she feels when she's around you*.

There are many different ways to make a woman feel good, which is why there are so many ways to approach women. You can make her horny (GM style); you can be funny and fun to be with (Game Show Host style); you can lead her imagination (patterning); you can form a personal connection and reinforce her beliefs and self-confidence (eliciting values, which we'll talk about soon). These are all valid approaches, but none of them will work if you don't show her that you are the kind of man that can show her a good time—and that's why confidence is the one key ingredient of any seduction situation.

Of course, clueless AFCs will make their own pitiful attempts at demonstrating value, but since they've never read this book, they have no idea how seduction works. The most common mistake is to try to be the non-threatening "nice guy," making her feel that she can talk to you like a brother. But you know what? Women don't have sex with their brothers!

Other AFCs, those who think they have looks going for them, assume that their mere presence and company is enough to make the girl wet. The value they're projecting, in other words, is big muscles and a pretty face. Believe me, these things are not of specific value to women. They may turn her on, and she may like the way she feels when she's standing beside you ("All the other girls are jealous! I must be good looking because he's good looking!"), but that's going to wear off fast if you don't demonstrate more concrete and long lasting values. Sure, being great looking will get you laid—but not nearly as much as knowing the secrets contained in this book.

Demonstrating the right kind of value—the kind the woman cares about—is the secret of the conversation. When you approached her, you didn't know her, so you just threw out a value (dirty, exciting, mysterious, funny) and hoped it would stick. That's a great starter. It showed you had something to offer, so it kicked open the door. Now it's time to learn to take her, that girl standing right beside you, to the unique place she and she alone wants to be.

Tonality

Before I tell you what to say and why, let's go over a few basics of conversation. These aren't taken from any books on persuasion or psychology, although you'll find a lot of these theories there, too. The difference is that what I'm going to tell you isn't a theory. It's been field-tested countless times, and it really works on real, live, gorgeous women!

Chump File: What's the Message I Am Sending?

Most AFCs don't understand that they need to demonstrate value to the woman (duh), so their approach really consists of nothing more than, "Here I am. This is the way I look. I hope you like me." Some AFCs assume this is enough because they're hot and any girl would fall for them just on looks. Others try to be "funny" and joke about the fact that they're not that good looking. Either way, it's a losing strategy. Anybody with half a brain and five minutes to think about the message they're actually sending, will see these approaches are for chronic losers only.

The first thing to think about is the way you say the words. If you're delivering a line, using one of the approaches I mentioned earlier, or even using a pattern from Ross Jeffries, you're running the risk of sounding like a phony or a pathetic clown delivering some pre-determined script. Obviously, that's not going to impress a woman.

In other words, it's not just what you say, it's how you say it that counts. You really have to believe what you're saying, whether it's a pick-up line or a question to try to get to know her better, and you have to convey that conviction.

It also helps not to sound like a loud-mouth, a jerk, or a mumbler; so use a soft, seductive voice and speak clearly. Don't overdo it—you'll sound like a phone sex operator—but a smooth, hypnotic delivery is an important element of seduction success. Remember, you're leading her with your voice, not just your words, so keep it smooth and stay on target.

In order to do this, you need to practice. Obviously, the best place to practice is with women, but don't be afraid to practice in the privacy of your own home as well, especially if you're a beginner. While pouring juice, taking a shower, cleaning your

"By talking about her, you learn more about her, which will be valuable to you in planning a strategy. . . . By not talking about yourself, you let your image speak for itself . . . the less women know about you, the more women want to know about you."

Don Diebel "America's #1 Singles Expert" (www.getgirls.com)

room (remember a PUA always keeps a tidy sex pad!), just act as if you're conversing with a woman. Say the words out loud, so that you begin to feel comfortable with your voice. If you have a recorder, go ahead and record yourself. Then listen to it and experiment with different modalities until you get it right. And no, it doesn't help to think the words—unless you plan on using ESP. Your voice is the medium, so practice it.

And never forget to use the "pregnant pause." A well-timed pause, right in the middle of a sentence, is the best way to create a sense of anticipation and mystery. You want her to be hanging on to your every word, right? Well, the pause is the way to create that feeling of breathless excitement.

Talking to Her = Echoing Her

A woman wants to be understood. In order for her to feel understood, you need not only listen to what she says, but feed it back to her. Yes, it helps if you agree with her, but it's not really nec-

Never disagree with a woman you're trying to seduce. If she's just heinous, bail. If, despite her idiocy, you decide to stick with your seduction plans, just keep smiling and nodding and echoing her ideas right back to her.

Romance Novels

Romance novels are garbage: laughable plots, boring dialogue, stilted relationships. But don't dismiss that garbage just yet because it's useful garbage if you want to seduce women. Why? Women love the "romantic" language in these books, so echo it back to them and they'll eat it up like candy. They won't know why, but your language will sound so right and so familiar, and suddenly they'll be wet and melted because of your ability to communicate in such a meaningful way.

So head out to the bookstore right now and hit the romance section. And while you're there, make sure to approach a honey bunny and ask her for a recommendation . . . for your sister, of course.

essary. Just listen to what she has to say, and feed it back to her later in the conversation. This is called echoing or verbal mirroring.

Be both subtle and creative with your feedback. A simplistic and immediate, "I completely agree with that. I think so, too!" will not do. You're working on a much more intimate level. Take what she says, paraphrase it, and present it as an original thought or opinion a few minutes later. Riff on the idea so that it sounds different, but portrays the same values and attitudes. Often, she won't remember she had previously said essentially the same thing, and therefore she "realizes" you have so much in common and share so many things that, surely, you're the man of her dreams. Even if she's not that dense, you're still showing her that you're listening and agreeing with her.

Echoing is even more powerful when you learn how to pick up on her "trance words"—the words she uses most often and that mean the most to her—and echo those back to her. This is a more complex idea, so we'll address that later on page 164. It's a very important idea, though, so feel free to jump ahead now and read all about it.

Controlling the Conversation

The number one rule of seduction conversation: make sure the conversation is going somewhere! Make sure everything you say has a purpose, that it's leading to . . . well, you know where you want this conversation to go: sex talk, intimacy, and then the chance to turn those words into action.

Lots of guys—all AFCs, of course—don't have a clue what they're trying to do when they talk to a woman. In fact, their mind-set is this: as long as I'm talking to her, that's a good thing! The longer I talk to her, the better my chances! So, they just pepper the poor woman with questions—"Where you goin'?" "What you doin'?" "What'd you do yesterday?"—that are nothing more than desperate small talk.

That is one of the worst mistakes. This kind of conversation is almost as bad as having no conversation at all. Unless, for some strange reason, she is already infatuated with you (and if you've only just met, she won't be), she'll be bored out of her mind. The problem isn't just in the approach, it's in the reason behind the approach. Spending as much time talking with the woman as possible will actually hurt your chances of success. You're just giving yourself an opportunity to say something wrong; you're creating the impression that you're desperate and have no place else to go; and, eventually, no matter how long you can keep afloat a conversation that only goes round in circles and has no real meaning to her, she's going to grow tired of you.

Remember: never leave the conversation because the girl is losing interest. Does this mean you should continue babbling even though she is quite obviously bored? No, this means you should have left *before* she was getting bored! Failing to exit at the right moment is one of the cardinal sins of seductive conversation. You should always leave at the high point of the conversation, when she's still fascinated by you. This will leave her wondering why you left so abruptly (as opposed to sighing in relief because she was so bored) and what else is so important in your life (you've obviously got a lot going on, she'll think). But, even more importantly, you'll leave her wanting more, which is the perfect state to leave a woman in, especially if you've already made the necessary arrangements (like extracting her phone number or agreeing to meet up later) to get in touch with her again soon.

The second mistake is the manner that the questions are being asked. Facts are boring. They aren't particularly personal, and they don't really have much meaning. You are after feelings and sensations. You want to get her thinking about her body and her emotions. Hopefully, this will elicit something that is special to her, something that makes her feel wonderful or full of longing or eager. When you find that thing, latch onto it—whether it's the rush of wind while she's ice skating or the thought of her new kitten licking her face. Now you're creating a personal bond based on her intimate beliefs or experiences.

You: So, tell me, do you have a favorite pastime—a hobby or a sport of some sort?

Her: Uh . . . well, I like to go ice skating.

You: Ah, I know exactly what you mean! Don't you just love that feeling of gliding and moving down the ice, hardly putting any effort into your movement, just going where momentum takes you? There's such grace, such beauty and freedom in the movement. And when you speed it up, then with almost every inch of your body you can feel the sensation of flying, and a slight breeze starting to blow. Me, I know I just absolutely love that feeling.

Her: Uh . . . yeah! (*wetting her lips*).

You: Yes, I can really tell you like that feeling of freedom, too!

In essence, you're just asking the age-old, boring question, "What do you like to do?" An AFC, though, wouldn't even bother listening to her reply, and would probably just continue

So What's Your Story?

We've already touched lightly on the open-ended approach, but we'll talk about it some more in the context of fluff talk. As much as I like sensation-based fluff talk, this is another smart technique, which is especially good for parties. Ask a woman, "So what's your story?" You're giving them an opening to talk about whatever they feel like talking about.

That's the brilliance of the question. It lets the woman pick the conversation. Whatever she chooses to talk about is something important to her. It may be an off-hand comment about her profession (office girl, architect, stripper) or it may be just how she got to this bar or party and who she knows. Doesn't matter. Just follow her lead and start asking questions. Whatever she's talking about is clearly the most interesting thing in the world to her—and now it's the most important thing to you. This creates instant rapport, which will soon turn into an intimate conversation.

Some girls will open up right away with something personal. They usually like to hear something personal back, so drop them some very general personal information about yourself that echoes what they've told you about themselves. They love this because it's basically saying, "I'm open and comfortable, you're open and comfortable, let's have a little fun."

If the woman doesn't respond, looks dazed and confused, or gives you a snippy answer and turns away, you better try another approach or hit the bricks fast. Why waste your time on that boring girl anyway?

The "story" approach also works on items of clothing or jewelry. For instance, you can simply walk up to a girl and say, "So, what's the story behind that necklace?" or "What's the story behind that beautiful scarf?" Just make sure the item is interesting and unusual. The item may not be special to her or have an interesting story, but if it's really unique she'll probably admire your attention to detail and open up.

with "Uh huh, great" because he was already thinking how to make his own favorite pastimes (drinking beer and watching sports) sound more interesting. Unlike that AFC, you were listening intently to what mattered to her and were able to create instant rapport based on her answer. Once you've established that you really understand her and connect to her, you can continue to explore what other kind of activities give her the same kind of sensation of complete freedom. And you know what one of those will end up being.

The question isn't just a conversation starter, it's a way to extract feelings and facts from the woman for use later. This in-between conversation, this filler, is called fluff talk. It's that gray area between the approach and actually getting into a meaningful conversation, and it's the bridge that can take you to another meaningful conversation after the first one ends. Fluff talk is essential to picking up women. It's the glue that fills in the blank spots and holds together your seemingly unconnected ideas.

In short, good fluff talk gives a directionless moment direction. You are searching out her feelings, trying to find that connection that will take you one step closer to your ultimate goal.

The Don'ts of Fluff Talk

> "Complaining or saying anything negative is kind of a turnoff. Some guys seem to think if they say that something sucks—the vodka, the music, the crowd—it shows they have an intelligent and critical eye. It just shows me he's a grump."
>
> —Wendy, Toronto

Being positive—and avoiding negativity at all costs—is one of the primary rules of fluff talk. The other is to never disagree with the woman. Here are a few more, as devised by old school PUA Don Diebel, "America's #1 Singles Expert" (www.getgirls.com):

- Personal (family, work, money) problems turn a woman off.

- Keep any sign of desperation out of your voice and your conversation.
- Watch the alcohol! Drunkenness really turns women off and makes a bad impression. Try not to drink, having, at most, a couple of drinks a night.
- Don't discuss her problems or offer advice.
- Previous girlfriends are forbidden territory—especially anything about how they mistreated you, dumped you, cheated on you, took you to the cleaners on child support, etc.
- If you aren't funny, don't try to be. A woman can sniff out your act. Just be friendly and smile (but make sure your smile looks sincere; guys that have a fake, pained smile plastered on their face for hours look insecure and just plain pathetic).
- Health problems and ailments—well, try to remember what you feel like when Uncle Horace discusses his gallbladder surgery.
- Generally, don't brag about yourself. While there are exceptions to the general rule, be very careful here. If you really have something impressive to talk about, you can let her in on it, but *only casually*. On the whole, women are good at sniffing out braggarts, and they don't like them (too many small penises in the bunch). And if what you're bragging about doesn't impress them, it's a complete turnoff. So be careful.
- Always talk about the woman and her interests.
- At all costs, avoid these three subjects: politics, religion, and conspiracy theories. They are guaranteed to nuke your otherwise wonderful interaction.

Body Language

Your body language is essential in making a connection with a woman. You need to show her you're strong, masculine, and caring, without being too forward. You want to create intimacy, but not push her too far. It might seem like a difficult line to walk, but once you've spent some real time with real women, it's not that hard to figure out how to make your body send all the right messages at the right time.

First of all, you should always stand or sit up straight. Slouching is for self-doubting schmos; you want to come across as confident and in control. Sure, there's a danger of looking like a tight-ass with a pinecone up your behind, but a friendly smile is the perfect antidote. Make it look natural; don't just stand there all stiff, really think about your posture and make it a natural part of your preparation routine. Good posture makes you appear taller and better looking.

When you approach a woman, you should always give her about two to three feet of room (unless the music is really loud or the bar is really crowded). As you talk with her, you should slowly close that gap by moving closer and closer to her. Inside eighteen inches is her personal space—you have to do some work before you can get in there, but once she lets you in without pulling back, stay there. That's your scoring zone.

A great way to create an expectation of intimacy is to enter her personal space occasionally, then pull back. For instance, within the first two minutes of conversation, lean forward as if you haven't heard what she says and lightly touch her on the back or shoulder. Stay there until she repeats what she said, then lean back and answer. You've created powerful intimacy, but because you had a good reason and were brief in your flirtation, you haven't crossed over and invaded her personal space.

And, of course, don't forget your kino—that's the touching part of the maneuver. There is nothing more powerful than an appropriate yet sensual physical touch. If the woman touches you, always touch her back in an equivalent place (this is called mirroring, and I'll talk about it more in the next section). If you're sitting down, always try to do a little foot flirting. Innocently brush your foot against her foot, while making eye contact with the girl. If she doesn't look away, do it again. You can throw in a teaser here, such as, "Are you foot flirting with me?" or you

The Head Tilt

Books on body language tell us that when a woman is interested in a conversation, she tilts her head. If you tilt your head when you listen to a woman, it helps to express to her that you're interested in what she's saying—even if you aren't. And it works even though the woman may not consciously realize that you're tilting your head. Next time a woman is talking about how the hot pink bridesmaid's dress that her best friend is forcing her to buy is a bad contrast with her naturally colored red hair, ask her the kind of follow-up questions that you normally would (about the friend, the dress, her hair, the wedding—wherever you are trying to lead the woman). This time, though, ask your follow-up with a slight tilt of your head. You'll find that you're much more effective in getting the woman interested because *she* senses that you're much more interested in her.

can simply let the action escalate on its own. And don't be surprised if in a few minutes her shoe is seductively hanging off her foot or her toes are giving you a crotch massage. Foot flirting (and touching or rubbing your thighs together if you're sitting next to each other) is a powerful aphrodisiac.

Mirroring

"I love it when a guy . . . mirrors my physical behavior, like when I'm sitting across from him and I lean in to say something, I like him to lean in . . . it makes me feel like we're in the same place. If I'm being a little frenetic and he's slow . . . I feel really far away."

—Carlie, Salt Lake City

We talked about echoing her attitudes and words, now let's talk about mirroring her physical movements and actions. This is probably something you've been doing all your life without realizing it; now it's time to put this power to work for you.

I'm sure you've noticed how people who are engaged in an interesting conversation—they are excited about what they are saying, what they are about to say, or what the other person is saying (in other words, they have rapport)—always seem to take the same poses and make the same movements. One leans forward and the other leans forward; one leans back and the other follows that lead. They cross their hands in the same manner and at the same time, tilt their heads simultaneously, seem to have similar side activities (he's playing with his keychain, she's punching the end of her pen). All their energy and concentration is on the conversation; everything else is happening unconsciously. Their minds are making a connection with each other, and their bodies are acting it out.

This similarity not only creates a bond, it creates a feeling of ease, comfort, understanding, and protection. You are together, mentally and physically. Isn't it obvious this is exactly what you want the woman to feel? By mirroring her, you can subconsciously make her feel all these wonderful feelings about you, and you'll develop instant rapport without even having to lift a finger (unless she lifts a finger and you mirror her).

Mirroring is about assuming the same posture as the girl, having the same facial expressions and even moving your hands in a similar manner to her. But mirroring isn't just a one-step process. There are three levels of power here, and once you get to the third level, you will be in total control of the seduction situation.

1. *Following*, or doing the movement after she does it, including body position, hand motions, and everything else she does. I know what you're thinking: this is crazy! I'm going to get caught! She must see me copying her! Don't listen to that little voice, fight it, because it is the voice of the Dark Side. Why? Because women *never*

notice! They just sense it unconsciously and become more comfortable, relaxed and (eventually) drawn to you.

2. *Pacing*, or doing the movements at the same time she does. Sounds impossible, right? Well, it isn't. In fact, if you've been following her and creating rapport, you will begin to pace each other almost automatically. In essence, your minds are picking up the stimuli from each other so fast that you are almost moving in tandem. Pretty great, huh? Well it gets even better, because pacing is merely a transition phase between following and doing what you came here to do: lead.

3. *Leading*, or having her imitate your movements. The first time this happens, it will blow you away. You are leading her, without her even knowing it! Cough and she coughs. Scratch and she scratches. In essence, because you're aware of the mirroring and putting effort into achieving it, your conscious mind is slowly gaining the upper hand on her unconscious mind. Usually, physical leading will keep pace with your verbal leading—as she gives in to the power of your voice and words, she will give in to the movements of your body as well. But sometimes physical leading can draw the woman in unconsciously before her conscious mind has given itself over to your verbal leading.

There is an even more advanced form of mirroring advocated by some experts in the seduction field. This is the mirroring of her breath and the blinking of her eyes. If you are able to do this effectively, it creates an extraordinary degree of rapport on a deeply unconscious level. But be warned: this is the highest level of mirroring, and it is better left to absolute fans of this art. If you're just starting out, or even if you're an advanced novice, you will most likely need to put too much concentration into checking her body for signs of breathing—and she is bound to think you can't keep your eyes off her breasts. The breast-check, by the way, is a huge "no-no!" with a woman, unless she already wants you, in which case things should be a lot further along than you still trying to mirror her breathing. Besides, all this concentration on her blinking and breathing just takes your much needed attention away from other more important things, like talking to her and listening to what she has to say.

Mirroring is great, but if it's distracting you from your primary objective—verbally creating a connection with the woman—then put it aside until you are ready to pick up this decidedly advanced tool and use it properly.

Calibrate the Girl

I've been talking about all the things you should do in any seduction situation, but there's one important rule I want to mention yet again because it's very important: always pay attention to her reactions and plan your next move based on them. If she's smiling or giving you that "come hither" look, then by all means keep trucking along; if she's yawning or frowning, you better change your approach fast.

Of course, these are extreme examples. Almost never will the green light and red light be this obvious. You're going to have to learn to read body language and facial expressions.

But how do you know what she's really thinking? Well, essentially, you ask. I call this calibrating the girl.

When you first start a conversation with a woman, always deliberately, but naturally in the flow of conversation, you say things that you know will get a positive and negative reaction—and then you look for how that reaction manifests itself.

For instance, if she says she has a cat, you might say, "What would you do if your cat got hurt?" Now watch the way her facial expression immediately changes and her posture shifts. Follow it up with something positive like, "I bet it's great when your cat comes in and wakes you up in the morning." Watch her closely for that unconscious reaction. These examples may sound silly—you may think you already know what happy and sad look like—but you'll find that the entire face and the entire body carry emotion, and this complex body language is what you are aiming to see. A poor AFC thinks that a smile or a frown conveys emotion, but you're looking for *all* of the signs that the girl gives off. Once you're in seduction mode (thirty seconds later) you just need to watch for those signs: they're mileposts on your ride to the promised land.

Of course, you can take a far less subtle approach, as suggested by Jake Thomson on ASF. Jake just flat out asks the woman to think of something she wholeheartedly, enthusiastically agrees with. Just have her think of it, but keep it a secret from you. Then he asks her to think of something she feels neutral about. Then something she wholeheartedly, enthusiastically disagrees with. Do this and you've calibrated the girl.

Pretty cheesy, right? Well, of course it is, so surely Jake has an angle. And he does, although it's pretty cheesy as well (but hey, seduction is first and foremost about having fun, so let's see what it's about). The angle is that Jake tells women that he's practicing to be a psychic. Now don't laugh, either now or when you try it on a girl. Women absolutely love this stuff; it connects directly with their hunger for mystery and intrigue. Pull out anything ESP, and you're guaranteed to have the full and complete attention of 99 percent of the women in the world—at least for a little while. And it's a great segue into gimmicks like palm reading or astrology, during which you can "read" her face as you "read" her future.

Reading Her Body Language

We covered the importance of your body language, now I want to talk about something equally important: reading her body language. As a conversation progresses, her body signs will subtly change and give you signals her conscious mind isn't prepared to give you yet. And not necessarily the positive kind either. Sometimes her body language will show very clearly that you're on the wrong track. Don't give up! She hasn't consciously ejected you yet. Just change your approach and watch her body for subtle signs.

The most important element of reading her body language is understanding whether she is "opening up" to you. In a social situation, most women (and men, too, so always remember to approach in an open posture!) begin in a closed defensive posture—arms crossed or close to the body between them and the stranger, legs together, body turned slightly away. But, as the conversation goes on and the tension eases, the woman's body should slowly shift to a more open posture—arms down or reaching out toward you, legs open, body turned toward you. If her posture is opening up to you, she's mentally opening up to you as well.

Below is a long list of other signals, both conscious and unconscious, to look for in a woman. The easiest way to understand these signals better is to watch for them in the conversations of others. Notice how two people interact and give each other signals. You'll learn a lot both about controlling your own body language and reading hers. And you'll have some fun, too. There's nothing funnier than seeing a guy, who seems to think his pick-up is so smooth and going so well, and knowing that, in fact, his doom is near because the woman isn't giving him any positive signals at all.

Signs of Interest

Her Mouth
- Her smile is big and relaxed, with upper and lower teeth showing.
- She bites the lower lip or shows her tongue (an especially good sign if it's pierced!)
- She wets her lips. Some women use a single lip lick; others run the tongue around the entire area.
- She puts her fingernail between her teeth.
- She pouts her lips while thrusting her breasts forward.
- She blows smoke straight out toward you, especially with pursed lips.

Her Eyes

- She keeps sneaking a peek at you.
- She holds your eye contact, even for a moment. When she looks away, she should look down instead of across the room.
- Her pupils are dilated.
- She raises and lowers her eyebrows, then smiles, usually with eye contact.
- She winks at you.
- She blinks more than usual, almost fluttering her eyelashes.

Her Hair

- She pushes her hand through her hair. This can be one motion or more of a general stroking, it doesn't matter.
- She twirls her hair around her finger while looking at you.
- She throws her hair back, off her shoulders.

Her Clothing

- Her nipples are getting perky. A great sign, but for God's sake don't get fixated on them! If you happen to notice, great.
- The hem goes up to expose some leg.
- She fixes, pats, or smooths her outfit.

Her Hands

- She exposes the palm of her hand.
- She rests her elbow in the palm of her hand, while holding out or gesturing with the other hand palm up.
- She lowers her drink. This is an invitation to come in closer.
- Her hands are steady and not fidgeting with keys, straws, glasses, etc.
- She rubs her wrists.
- One hand touches one of her breasts.

- She touches her cheek briefly. If she leaves her hand there, it's a bad sign.
- She plays with her jewelry, especially with a stroking or light pulling motion. If she's pinching or yanking, it's a bad sign.
- She touches you while talking.
- She looks away and pretends to check her watch as you pass her.

Her Voice

- She raises or lowers the volume of her voice to match yours.
- She either speeds or slows her speaking to match your pace.
- She laughs in unison with you.
- In a crowd, she speaks only to you and focuses her undivided attention on you.

While Seated

- She moves in tune with the music, with her eyes on you.
- She straightens her posture, and her muscles appear to tense.
- Her legs open.
- Her legs rub against each other.
- Her leg rubs against the table leg.
- Her crossed leg is pointed toward you. Often, she will rock it gently toward you as well.

Other

- She mirrors your body language and body position.
- Her skin reddens, especially her ears or cheeks.
- She leans over and whispers in her friend's ear, just like junior high.
- She stands with her head cocked at a slight angle, one foot behind the other, hips thrust slightly forward.

She Just Keeps Talking!

What happens if you're about to launch into your spiel, to really knock her socks off and she starts talking and talking and talking and just won't stop? Is this is a good sign? You bet it is. Just smile knowingly and let her talk her little heart out. As soon as the topic of sex comes up, you know you've got her. Just lay back, be friendly, don't say too much and let her talk herself right into your bed.

- You keep bumping into her "accidentally" or you catch her glancing at you. Or, more subtly, she may just happen to keep putting herself near you over the course of ten or twenty minutes.

But be warned: although these signals work with most beautiful women, the really gorgeous, knock-out model types very seldom bother to display any such signs of interest at all. Why? Because they've never had to, so they've never learned them, either consciously or unconsciously. With these women, you have to be alert for the more subtle signs of interest.

The best sign a gorgeous woman is interested in you: she looks at your face. Average girls will look at your face all the time, then if she's interested she'll move on to more overt signals. Gorgeous women don't have to use overt signals, so if she keeps looking at your face, even just from time to time, this is all the sign you're going to get—and all the sign you should need.

Common Signs of Interest:
The Female Perspective

Here's a list of common signs of interest from the female point of view, as told by an actual female, Stephanie Alexander. I love her attentiveness and confident attitude. I wonder what her body's like . . .

- *She pays you a compliment.* Men usually compliment women, not the other way around. If she gives you a compliment, it usually means that she's interested.

- *She's arguing but smiling.* Disagreeing, but doing it flirtatiously, as in "Oh, you can't fool me that quickly!" means she's interested in you. If a woman isn't interested, she'll give a dull "uh-huh" instead.

- *She tells you when she can't hear you.* If she's asking you to repeat yourself, she wants to hear what you have to say, even if there's pounding house music in the background. If you suggest talking somewhere that's quieter, she'll be interested.

- *Your lame jokes get a laugh.* Either she's drunk on you or she's just drunk.

- *She's eager to touch you.* Touch her back! Don't accelerate the action; just mirror it back to her.

- *She waits for you.* If you go off to the bathroom and she hasn't wandered off with her friends or another guy, she's interested. If you wait for her, she'll sense the same from you.

- *She doesn't pull away.* If you lean into her personal space to grab something (drink, ashtray, etc.) and she doesn't flinch, she feels at ease with you.

- *She wants to know where you're headed when you leave.* Even if she doesn't join you (she can't abandon her friends, doesn't feel safe with a stranger, etc.), she probably will at a later date.

Being Interested

You must always appear, in any conversation with a woman, to be interested and fascinated by what she's saying and who she is. But do you know what's even better? Actually being interested!

It not only makes the pick-up easier, it makes you a better person and her a lot more fun to be around.

Always keep your outcome in mind. You're not after Ms. Right, you're after Ms. Right Now. That means you should be able to find a girl with different values than yours fascinating, or even an airheaded bimbo entertaining. This isn't a life commitment; it's just some fun. And if you like what you see, hear, and get, who knows, maybe that one night turns into a lot more. But that only comes later!

Remember, there is something wonderful about every girl, even besides the fact that she's female. So, if you concentrate on finding it, you'll be a much happier person—and you'll get laid a lot more often, too.

CHAPTER 10

Eliciting Values

Eliciting Values Explained

The point of eliciting values is to find out what she wants in and from a man . . . and then to turn into the man of her dreams by providing it for her.

The secret, in other words, is not to be a dream man (a beginner PUA strategy), but *her* dream man. A woman likes to feel that she's unique, that she has something you don't see in other women, and that's what makes her attractive to you. You create this feeling by focusing on her and asking her deep meaningful questions that really probe her life and thoughts.

And you'd better be paying attention when she's talking, not letting your thoughts wander to that meeting you have tomorrow or the extraordinary pointiness of her breasts. This is critical because, in a few minutes, you're going to feed those values back to her—and reference them all back to yourself. This technique, which in many ways forms the basis of the seduction conversations, is called "eliciting values."

The best way to find out her values is, simply, to ask her.

You: So, if I were to ask you what's important to you in a relationship, what would you say?
Her: I like tall guys.

You: Well, I'm not very tall, so I guess you're not interested in me . . .

Wrong. Wrong. And wrong. You couldn't be making a bigger mistake. You've been fooled by the oldest misunderstanding in the book. What that woman just gave you was what we'll call a "means value"—in other words, a physical characteristic. It's not tallness that she's after, it's the *feeling* a tall man gives her when he's by her side. The same is true of good-looking guys, which is why good looks aren't the only thing—or even an important thing. They're merely worthless means values, so don't go out and get leg implants if you're short or rob a bank to become financially secure.

The important part is not what she says she wants (tall guys, rich guys); the important part is the feeling she experiences when she is around those guys (safety, security). That's what you're after, because that's what she's after.

So let's go over that last exchange again.

You: If I were to ask you what's important to you in a relationship, what would you say?
Her: I like tall guys. (*means value*)
You (*nodding*): And what do you experience when you're with a tall guy?
Her: It just makes me feel safe and protected.

Bam! You've just moved from a means value with no seductive power, to what we'll call an "End Value" (also known as a "Desired State"), that is the key to unlocking her heart . . . or unhooking her bra, or both. Now, as long as you can create those feelings of safety and protection (or whatever she indicates) in her mind, she will associate those feelings with you—then you're well on your way to becoming her dream man.

Understanding Values

Don't go rushing in yet. She's given you her Desired States, but let's be honest . . . you still don't have a clue what she's after.

> Do not try to create a market for your product just because you think it's a great product. Find a product that the market demands, and you will be successful. Fill a need, and you can't go wrong.
>
> —from *Sweep Women off Their Feet and into Your Bed*

She told you she values honesty, but what does that mean? That you always tell her the truth? Should you blurt out, then, that you're a PUA sex machine looking for another pick-up? Doubtful. Very doubtful.

You need context. What does honesty really mean *to her*? And more importantly, why does she value it? If you just go charging off and using your own assumptions about what her values mean, then you're liable to fall into a trap of your own devising. Or, as Jake Thomson put it on ASF, "If you hallucinate that you understand what honest, kind, and respectful means to her, you've got a better chance of eating a can of beans and farting your way to the moon."

So, before you go rushing in, you need to step back and explore her End Values a little further. Why does she want security above other things in her relationship? There's almost always a reason. A friend of mine kept getting negged by a beautiful blond flight attendant, until he finally gave her the sense of security she was after. That's when he learned she had been attacked by four guys with guns in college and had dated tall guys ever since. She wound up, a few years later, marrying an FBI agent. He was only about 5′6″ tall, but she felt safe.

Is it always that easy or clear? No, but it is more times than you think. And you know what, if somebody elicited values from you, there's probably a reason for your lusts, too. We're only human, after all, and our desires are usually based on our past experiences. That's why they say men always want to replace their mothers, and women always want a man like

---

The Three Steps to Nirvana

Step 1: Understand that all people, including supermodels and ultra-gorgeous women, have unfulfilled desires. Even Bill Gates wishes he could do something differently; even Elle MacPherson finds herself *wanting* sometimes. They ache for something, crave something . . . and that's the same craving that drives all women, from dog-faced wallflowers to ultra-gorgeous glamour queens. They may have an army of suitors, they may be sleeping on the finest satin sheets, but they ache for adventure, or freedom, or respect, or pampering, or feeling like a little girl again. It's always *something*.

   Step 2: Find out what she aches for. Be sensitive. You can pick this up with small clues that leak out over time, or with an understanding and respectful direct question. Just be intelligent and structure your questions in ways that uncover these nice pieces of data. You're looking for something she's always wanted, but isn't getting right now.

   Step 3: Fill the void and anchor that fulfillment to (guess who?) . . . you.

---

daddy. That's why I often go back to her childhood. I find out what she missed out on or what she wanted then, and it almost always leads directly to what she is missing out on now.

   And then, of course, I fill that hole in her life (no pun intended).

Trance Words

While you're eliciting values, you should also be listening on a closer level for the actual words she's saying. The words she often repeats or puts particular emphasis on are her so-called Trance Words. These are the words she thinks with and is most

A Values Analysis

Jobet Claudio, a Mindlist subscriber, was getting nowhere with a woman—until he found out what she wanted. He found out that her father had died when she was young. Using that information, he was able to give her the feeling that she wanted: "I took that tack and talked about how good it feels to be a little girl sitting on daddy's lap and embracing him, and asking for small 'gifts' and things like that. Gosh . . . it worked." That strategy worked, but it might have worked even better if he had taken the time to further explore her values. Asking about her father, especially small clues—his voice, his mannerisms, what he used to do with her—would have revealed more about what she was looking for. Using that information, this PUA could have shown the woman that he could offer her what was missing from her life. His actions wouldn't have been sneaky or dishonest—he would have found what she was looking for and given it to her.

familiar with. By remembering them and subtly repeating them back to her, you are tapping directly into her subconscious mind. She won't know why, but she'll feel like you completely understand her, that you're "on the same wavelength," or even, sometimes, that you're soul mates. Whatever you do, and whatever you say, is much more likely to be understood and appreciated because you've bound her to you—just by using a few words!

Once you pick up on a Trance Word, you should repeat it back to her in a slightly different way. Then you should file it away in your memory and use it again a little later in the conversation. Use it two or three times—don't overdo it, but just make sure it sticks in her subconscious mind.

You: So what's important to you in a relationship?
Her: I want a man who makes me feel comfortable.

You: I love being with people who make me comfortable so I can let my guard down and really open up to them.
Her: (*some reply*)
You (*looking around*): I like this place. It's very comfortable. That's one of the qualities I look for in a coffee shop, a place where I can just relax and enjoy who I'm with.

Trance Words are an incredibly powerful tool. And they're incredibly easy to use, right? Actually, they do take a little getting used to. All this listening and filing can sometimes throw off your rhythm and leave the conversation stalled. But once you learn to automatically recognize and record Trance Words, you'll find yourself making connections without even thinking about them.

Anchors

Anchoring is a based on the classic Pavlovian Response, a reflex first explored and made famous by the Russian scientist Pavlov. In his experiment, Pavlov rang a bell and at the same time offered a dog some food. When the dog saw and smelled the food, he started to salivate. Pavlov repeated this many times over a period of days, always getting the dog to salivate at the sight and smell of the food. Then he rang a bell without offering the dog any food. As soon as he heard the bell, the dog started salivating. Pavlov had programmed a conditioned response (the thought of food when a bell rang), which would create the positive reaction, even when the object of desire wasn't offered!

Is a woman like a dog? You bet she is! Your goal as a pick-up artist is to get her salivating at the thought of you. You want to keep her on a constant high, laughing and feeling great about herself (and by extension you), but, of course, even for the most experienced pros, that's easier said than done.

That's where anchoring comes in. You want to create a positive Pavlovian response, even when there's no reason for her to feel happy. But how do you ring the bell? Easy. Every time you see a girl light up with delight, smile, laugh, or just feel damn

The Verbal Anchor

Anchors aren't just physical. They can be verbal, too. Don't believe me? Try this experiment. Whenever your girl is about to cum, whisper a specific phrase in her ear (for instance, "Oh yes, do it!" or "That's my girl!"). Repeat this process three times. Now the next time you're out in public, at the most embarrassing time, lean over and whisper those words in her ear. She'll turn bright red from a wave of passionate lust every time.

good because of the wonderful feelings you are creating for her, *touch her in a specific place* (on the hand, the shoulder, the elbow, inside the lower arm). When you touch her, say something like, "It's a great feeling, isn't it?" This will distract her from your touch, because you don't want her focusing on your movements, you want her to feel it unconsciously. This also reinforces the physical anchor with a verbal anchor. You keep saying it feels great, so something must feel great! But what is it? She doesn't know, but she knows she likes it!

Once you've touched her in the same way three times, you've set an anchor. Now when you touch her there again—with the same pressure, the same motion, etc.—you will suddenly and unexpectedly evoke in her the feeling of happiness and excitement that she experienced when you planted the anchor. In other words, you just rang the bell; she's salivating. Really good, experienced PUAs can plant anchors for different feelings all over her body—laughter on her shoulder, excitement on the elbow, romance on the back, and horniness on the knee.

But be careful! Don't overuse your anchors because you will eventually desensitize her to them. Ring the bell ten times without food, and the dog will stop salivating. Same with a woman, which is why you should only use your anchor two or three times without replanting it with some more actual feelings of happiness and horniness.

Anchors are best established early in the conversation, when she's on a high and you're making her feel special and attractive (and attracted to you). Sooner or later, for whatever reason (she's tired, worried, there's a natural lull in the conversation), her mood will droop. Fire off an anchor and you'll bring her right back up to where you want her to be—with almost no effort on your part.

Introducing the Questions

If you simply ask a girl, "What's the most important thing for you in a relationship?" it might sound a little forward. But what if you couched it as a hypothetical, such as, "If I were to ask you what's the most important thing for you in a relationship, how would you describe it?" This gives the woman a little more distance from the question, and helps her think of her answer as more of a philosophical response than a deep personal insight (which it always is). You are asking the same, overly-forward question, but you are doing it in a way that lets the woman stay comfortable.

A cheap psychological trick? Absolutely. But it got you in the door, so run with it. Here are a few strategies:

The curious approach. Talk about how important it is for you to get to know people (not just women), how you love to hear about what other people are thinking. "I think it's an absolutely fantastic feeling to get to know another human being, especially what someone else thinks about major issues revolving around us in the world . . . or even just their own personal feelings. I find that very stimulating. I mean, if I were to ask you what you really value in a relationship, what would you say?" And remember, that "major issues around the world bit" is total bunk. You are going to avoid politics *at all costs* and head straight for her feelings!

The no BS approach. Address the fact that you're going to dig deep into her psyche up front, and play it off like as a point of connection. "You know, in most situations like this, a person will ask, 'So how are you doing?' or ask you about what you did this weekend. It's not that I'm not interested in that, I enjoy it, but I find that I get a lot more out of people by talking on a deeper level, really penetrating into their lives. Is there something that challenges you in your life, maybe in your work or in your personal relationships?"

The important issue. If you're on an interesting subject but not heading in the right direction (her interior thoughts and feelings), then act a little confused and really laser in on the right stuff. "I understand what you're saying, but you've got to ask yourself: what's important to you in . . . (relationships, work, men, friends, whatever you're talking about)?" If she doesn't take that bait, rephrase the question. "Alright, let me ask you then: what's really important to you in . . . ?"

The ask her to explain approach. If she says something you totally disagree with, don't challenge her—use it! Tell her you hadn't thought of things that way, and ask her to explain her reasoning. If she hesitates (she may take a bit of offense thinking you're being a smart-ass), say, "No, seriously, I'm very curious. What was the moment or experience that convinced you?" She not only will tell you something important to her, she may even give you the best way to change her mind about *anything*.

The boy toy approach. This is a dangerous, dangerous approach, but I'm including it because it's perhaps the best way to get to the most important of her values: what she looks for in a man. Basically, you bring up her relationships . . . and *hope* she doesn't have a boyfriend. As we'll learn later, you never want to give the woman an opening to think about or (especially) mention her boyfriend. So be warned!

You: Do you like living here/hanging out here?
Her: Yeah, I guess.
You (*flirty*): What do you like to do for fun? Do you have a lot of guys chasing you?

Her: Not really. I'm picky. [This is her bitch shield coming up as
a blocker—use it to your advantage.]

You: Really? Well then, what qualities do you look for in a guy?

Gimmicks

I'm not a fan of gimmicks in general, but they can be useful in
certain situations. Don't rely on these exclusively; you still need
to develop your ability to start and control a conversation.
They're a great way to mix things up, however, and often they're
a whole lot of fun.

The "I Like" Game

Some guys use this as an opener, but I think it's better as a
way to move from fluff talk to eliciting values. Whenever the
appropriate time comes up, just drop in, "I like Prodigy" (if their
music is playing) or "I like Arizona" (if she's just been on a trip).
Then follow up with another group or state that you like. When
she looks at you funny, say, "What do you like?" She'll usually
answer you back with a similar topic. Hit her back, and watch
her respond. Now swiftly, but with a big smile, start moving
her around to different topics, like food, movies, etc. Your goal
is to eventually get her into an interchange of personal and
romantic ideas and things that create positive feelings ("I like
a hot shower" or "I like finding $20 in my pocket when I
didn't know it was there."). If you're a pro, you may even get
into the sex talk.

Here are a few great examples for the "I like" game. I like . . .

- Laughing so hard my face hurts.
- Hearing my favorite song on the radio.
- Hot towels out of the dryer.
- Finding a great shirt in the bargain bin.
- Playing with puppies.

- Late night phone calls that last for hours.
- Chocolate milkshakes with a straw for each of us.
- Getting butterflies in my stomach every time I talk to someone.
- Having someone tell me I'm good looking.

The Question Game

Another favorite is to just say, "Let's play the Question Game!" What is it? Truth or dare without the dare, essentially. If she agrees, you can ask her anything you want about herself. But remember to ask about her feelings and important experiences, not what she had for breakfast. And don't go overboard on the sexual questions. Ease her into the game and then later ask her one of the following, "What was your first kiss like?", "When did you have sex for the first time?", "How did you first orgasm?", "What makes you horny?" If she answers positively— that is with honesty and a smile—follow up with the more intimate question, "Would you like to kiss me?"

The Finish My Sentence Game

In this variation on the Question Game, you say the first part of the sentence and she finishes it. Start with simple, factual questions, but move quickly to more interesting (and useful) territory, such as "I feel an incredible connection with a man when . . .", "I feel excited when . . .", "I am most comfortable with . . .", "I feel good when . . ." You're giving her the opening to flirt with you, so when you see her drifting toward sexual answers, make your way toward the coup de grâce, "I feel absolutely turned on when . . ." and then, before she can answer, lean over and plant a huge kiss on her mouth.

Remember, none of these games will work if you haven't already built rapport. They're not solutions, just shortcuts. As always, if you can't read her body language and use her answers in your follow-up, these games won't be productive.

The Questions

Before you can lead a woman toward a desired state, you must get her to divulge the feelings and emotions that are important to her. The question, "Do you value excitement in your life?" is worthless; "What excites you?" is the question you should be asking.

There are nine important questions to get answered about the woman when eliciting values. You don't (and shouldn't) phrase them this way, but these are the End Values that will be most useful to you. And no, you don't have to discover all nine! In most cases, two or three will do:

1. What does she want?
2. What does she like?
3. What does she think she needs?
4. What does she think she deserves?
5. What did she have before that she wishes she had now?
6. What did she have before that she really wants to avoid?
7. What scares her?
8. What makes her happy?
9. What makes her horny?

The following questions will elicit specific responses, set the mood, and start you on the trail of the End Values. They'll help you get to know the woman and put her in an altered state by making her dig for answers deep with her conscious and subconscious.

1. What do you like most about your line of work?
2. What is the most unusual thing you've ever done? (Hopefully, she'll come up with some sexual stuff. If not, you can come back later with a more pointed probe.)
3. What one trait would your friends use to describe you?
4. What do you think I'm like? (Good for useful feedback— and possibly a little wish fulfillment. Watch her closely here!)

Never get *too* excited about the activities she partici[...]
or the values she says she cherishes. That just makes i[...]
like you have no life. Instead, just ask her some intell[...]
questions and echo back her feelings.

5. What's your first childhood memory? (Even if it's not positive, she'll open up to you.)
6. What's your most pleasant memory from school? (Hopefully, it's something to do with a guy. If not, follow up and try to make it sexual.)
7. In what period of your life were you most popular? (Have her remember the good times.)
8. What was the happiest moment in your life? (Hopefully sexual and, if so, follow up ASAP. She may be flirting with you.)

As always, it's important to understand her reaction. If she doesn't respond positively or enthusiastically to your line of questioning, try a new track. When she latches on to something, take her deeper into the feeling and experience by asking her more detailed, intricate questions. You are forcing her to really remember those feelings, to live in that moment. Suggest other possible outcomes that will drive her closer to where you want to be. If you have created connection and rapport, she will be more than happy to open up to you, and thrilled by the fact that you're listening and going there with her.

If the answer to a question is not sufficient for your needs (You: "What scares you?" Her: "Mice."), ask her to elaborate or explain her answer in a follow-up question. And if there's anything you don't understand—and remember you can never understand with one question what a woman means by honesty, passion, etc.—then ask another question to quantify her answer. Don't think you understand her; be sure you understand her. That is the only way of:

1. Making her feel completely understood by you
2. Completely understanding her

These are the two conditions you need to become her Mr. Right.

The Right and Wrong Way to Elicit Values

Once you're in the zone with the woman and finding out some good quality information, never break that momentum by asking disconnected questions. If you're changing the topic, you have to do it by asking her tangential questions that flow from her answers. Here's a great example, based on one by NYC (ASF), of how to move the topic around without losing control of the conversation:

The Right Way

You: Where do you work?
Her: I'm a public school teacher.
You: The kids must be rowdy.
Her: Oh, they're sometimes hard to control
You: I was out of control, too, sometimes. When I was a kid . . . [Offer her a story from your childhood—keep it rowdy but not scary so that she can relate; something like, "my friends and I used to steal beers from our parents, sneak out at night and get up to trouble," etc.]
Her: I did the same thing! [Make sure that you listen attentively.]
You: How old were you?
Her: Fourteen. I was too young to . . . [Keep listening.]
You: Did you live with both your parents?
Her: No, they divorced when I was ten.
You: That sounds hard. How did you feel when they split up?
Her: It was lonely and scary, but . . . [Keep listening!]
You: That happened to a close friend of mine. She likes to be by herself . . .
Her: I do, too. I can't stand having a roommate . . .

The Wrong Way

You: What do you do?

Her: I'm a public school teacher.

You: Did you live with both of your parents when you were a kid?

Her: No, they divorced when I was ten.

You: Do you live by yourself?

Her: What's with the fucking Twenty Questions!?

Becoming the Man She Wants

You've elicited her values. Now it's time to put them to work. You know what she wants, both her End Values and her Means Values. You know her Trance Words. You've let her talk on and on about herself; now it's time to focus the attention back on you.

Do not simply state her likes back to her. In fact, don't ever tell a woman anything directly; there's no mystery in that. It will just sound awkward, and there's a good chance she'll see through your scheme—especially if you're not being very subtle or tossing out her Trance Words and wish list too rapidly.

The key is to tell her stories about yourself that demonstrate the values she finds attractive and pleasurable. If earlier she had mentioned she likes cats, then tell a story in which you demonstrate that you love cats. (And no, you don't have to love cats, fool! You're playing to her desires.) That's an easy example, but the same holds true for a woman who values comfort and familiarity. Tell a story that not only makes you seem comfortable and familiar to her, but shows you value comfort and familiarity, too.

If she likes cats, your "comfort" story could involve cats. And say "comfortable" and "familiar" at least twice in the story. And when she smiles, touch her on the elbow like you did before when eliciting her positive memories.

That's the complete seduction package: End Values, Means Values, Trance Words, and Anchors. If she's not feeling heart-pounding rapport with you, and if she's not transported to the

Some chicks like aggressive men and some like passive men that they can cuddle with and eventually have sex with. Find out first which one she wants and then project that image at her.

—NYC (on ASF)

exact state of excitement that would make her want to get to know you better, there's something wrong with your technique—or something wrong with her.

Time Distortion

There's a right way to tell a story (make it about a "friend," reinforce the fact that you share her values) and a wrong way to tell a story (brag, have no idea what her values are). Time distortion is one of the right ways.

Girls love to dream . . . so dream with them. Use these dreams to create intense emotions and link them all to you—talk about your favorite fantasies, like walking hand-in-hand on the beach with that special someone, or making out under a tropical waterfall. This is risqué sex talk, especially with a girl you barely know, but she'll have little resistance to participating with you because it's all perfectly safe. After all, it's only a fantasy.

The key to linking this fantasy to you, along with all the powerful and positive emotions you've created, is to use time distortion. You're not just describing some hypothetical event, you're talking about something that is going to take place six months in the future—next spring, summer, winter, whenever is appropriate! And you're not going to be in this fantasy alone, you're going to be there with *that special someone*. If you've worked up enough rapport (and you should because you've already elicited her values), then the fact that she is that special someone should be obvious without your having to say it.

Ask questions and elicit values *before* you tell a woman anything about yourself. When you do finally start telling her
about yourself, you'll know what to play up and what not to
mention, because you'll know what she sees as a positive and
a negative.

   Since you'll know what traits she wants in a sex partner,
you'll be able to portray yourself as that perfect sex partner.
She'll keep thinking about all of the great characteristics you've
shown her. Because you've found out what she wants before
you talk with her, you can tailor your image to fit her desires.

And I don't need to tell you, since you now know her values,
that this should be a fantasy that fulfills her every wish and
desire! Time distortion should only be tried when you know
how she's going to respond. If you already know the woman a
bit, you can try something like the following:

You: I love traveling, and I'd love to go on a trip next year. If you
    had to choose one place to travel to, anywhere in the world,
    next winter, where would it be?
Her: I guess I'd like to travel to Switzerland.
You: Switzerland . . . what do you see yourself doing there?
Her: Skiing . . . the mountains . . . relaxing . . .
You: Would you like to sit by a warm fire at the end of the day,
    next to someone special, feeling the warmth spreading
    through your muscles, feeling the relaxation . . .
Her: That sounds comfortable.
You: Someone could massage your shoulders, working his way
    slowly down your back, and the two of you could slip into a
    warm, comfortable hot tub, feel the heat . . .

When it works, man, it is powerful. You may have known
her only six minutes, but after a "walk on the beach" together

---

Rich Bitch

You've elicited values, and you've found out that . . . well, she's a greedy money-grubber only interested in the deep pocket boys. And you don't have five dollars to your name. Give up? Hell, no! This is where time distortion comes in. You've got to sell her on the idea that you have a plan to make a lot of money (you've got a business, right?), and then, before she has a chance to think about it too hard, start laying on the fantasy of what it will be like with *that special someone* once you've got all that money, those cars, that giant marble bathtub. Use your anchors to link all these ideas to you and the way you make her feel. For instance, touch her elbow when you mention what you will be able to buy. Most of the time, your "business plan" doesn't even have to make sense. She'll be eating out of your hand just at the thought of the fantasy you spun for her.

---

she'll feel like you've known her for six months. And then just watch her eyes light up when you ask for her phone number.

The Perfect Relationship

This is a classic eliciting values scheme. It's so simple, it's almost guaranteed to work. Almost.

Step 1

You: What is important to you in a relationship?
Her: Well . . . [answer 1] . . .
You: What lets you know that you have [answer 1]?
Her: (*She talks.*)
You: What else is important to you in a relationship?
Her: [answer 2]

You: I see . . . [talking about answer 2]
Her: (*She continues talking.*)
You: Is that all? What else is important to you?
Her: Actually, [answer 3] is very important to me.

Step 2

You: Of those three things—[answers 1, 2, and 3]—which is the
most important? What's vital to you?
Her: Well . . . I guess [answer *x*]
You: Why is [answer *x*] important?
Her: (*She talks.*)
You: Of the other two, which is most important?
Her: [second answer]

Step 3 (About an Hour Later)

You: I think that we could really have something wonderful
together since we have [answers 1, 2, and 3, in the order of
her preference]. Do you feel how great this could be?

CHAPTER **11**

Troubleshooting

Why Do You Ask?

Asking all these questions can sometimes result in the woman getting defensive. The most common sign of this is her asking, "Why do you ask?" You're taking her some place she doesn't feel comfortable going, and she's throwing up a blocker.

So be honest. And no, don't tell her you're eliciting values because you're trying to pick her up, dumbass! Tell her what you're really doing: trying to get to know her so that you can find out whether she is the type of person you should bother spending time with. There's no way she can argue with that logic, right?

And don't be afraid to run some positive reinforcement of her feelings for you here. When you ask a woman what she values in a relationship, and she asks you why you want to know, you don't have to actually answer her question. Instead, respond with something similar to this: "I enjoy getting to know women, especially women who seem intelligent, caring, and emotionally open. It's wonderful to feel close to a woman like that."

You've just made her feel close to you, and better about you, while avoiding her question. In other words, you've used what could have been a blocker for an AFC as an opportunity to get that much closer to unzipping her pants. That's why you're a PUA.

Are You Trying to Seduce Me?

Often, a woman will pick up on the fact that you are a smooth, confident operator, and then try to pin you to the wall. I've heard the following questions countless times, and almost always with a sly smile from the woman:

- Are you trying to seduce me?
- So you enjoy seducing women?
- Have you broken many hearts?
- You're a player, aren't you?

What do you do? Deny it and become defensive? Or admit it and risk making her feel like she's just another notch on your long leather belt of love? The answer, of course, is neither. The best way to deal with these questions is to avoid answering them all together, just as you avoided answering, "Why do you ask?" In fact, I recommend using the same approach that was recommended for the "Why do you ask?" question.

The problems of trying another answer (whether yes or no) is that you have no idea what the woman wants. Being a lady's man is a good thing with some women: they like a guy with experience that knows how to have a good time. This is especially true of older women; they have no time or desire to train a younger man. With other women, however, knowing that you're a PUA makes them feel that they're not special, that they're just another piece of meat. Most women want a man who's had a few partners, and enough experience to be good in the sack, but isn't a player.

In other words, your best bet, as always, is to remain a mystery. Divert their attention, make them feel special, and let them imagine you in their minds as exactly the kind of man they want to be with.

If you get stuck, try a few of these:

- I think you're a fascinating woman, and I'd like to get to know you better.
- There's something about you that draws me to you.
- I think that I'm the kind of person that might have a great time with a person like you.

Have You Ever . . . ?

Asking a woman "Have you ever . . . ?" and then following up with a positive experience or feeling is the basis of Speed Seduction®. It's also an important part of pacing her reality, because you're trying to take the woman to that place of pleasure and excitement—and what better way to get there than painting her the picture?

And what happens if she refuses to play along? For instance, you ask her, "Have you ever felt the wind in your hair, you know, how it makes you feel so free and uninhibited?" and she answers with a simple, "No."

There are two explanations for that response, and neither is very promising. The first is that she's young, inexperienced, or unimaginative and truly can't comprehend what you're talking about. This doesn't disqualify her from your radar screen, but it will probably make for a rather dull night. (Unless she's a kino girl!)

The second, and more likely scenario, is that she's trying to blow you off. Don't let her dissuade you! Instead, switch to the third person and describe the feeling you want her to have just as it was told to you by a female friend. And yes, this female friend is a myth, but who is ever going to be the wiser?

You: Have you ever met someone and instantaneously felt such a complete attraction for him that you just had to do something about it?

Her: No.

You: Well, I guess different people have different experiences, because my friend Lola was just telling me about an experience just like that. She was in a coffee shop, just like this one, and a man walked in. He was average looking, but there was something about him, about his intensity when he looked at her . . . that let her know that she had to get to know him better.

Age Difference

Age difference should never be a problem, and you should never approach a woman as if it were a problem. You are the perfect man for this woman, and that's exactly what you're going to prove to her right now. Looks aren't a problem. Money isn't a problem. So why should age even come up?

But of course it does, and it's sometimes a problem. But let's make something perfectly clear: it's her problem, not yours.

Being "too young" is rarely a problem. Older women are at the very least flattered by the attention, and often eager to experience your hot, young action. Being "too old" is a much more serious issue, especially when it comes to the newly legal (girls in their late teens and early twenties). These women aren't experienced enough to understand the pleasures of an older man, and they often have an inflated view of the importance not just of themselves, but of their age group as well. Some twenty year olds will dismiss you if you're over twenty-six. Please! These women have no idea what they're missing.

There are those who advocate lying. Once you've slept with her and shown her a good time, then let her in on your real age as if it's the biggest secret in the world . . . something your mom doesn't even know.

I disagree. It's one of my fundamental pieces of advice to never lie to a woman (for one thing, it's too hard to remember all the different lies) and age is no place to start. There's a much better way.

Of course, you'd never bring up the age difference yourself, so when she brings it up listen to the way she says it. Is she being playful? Is she hesitating? Or is she using it as an excuse to blow you off?

If it's one of the first two, then simply reframe her question and feed it back to her in a positive way, then follow up with some time distortion about all the positive aspects of being with an older man. Keep talking until you've convinced her! If you let her butt in too soon, you're only setting yourself up for a fall.

Her: Aren't you a little old for me?

You: I am older than you, but just imagine how many things I've learned in all those years. I mean, it's a winning situation either way. If we just become friends, then I can share with you my wisdom. If we become more than friends, then I can show you what I'm talking about. In six months, I could show you so many things: a quiet moonlit night on the beach where I like to go . . .

If she's being bitchy about the age difference (some women will act like you're a perv) and really throwing up the shield, then you have to act fast and turn the equation around on her by questioning her maturity.

Her: How old are you?

You: Forty.

Her: Don't you think you're a little old for me? You could be my father!

You: You're right. It is tough finding girls your age that are mature. Do you feel mature enough to be with an older man?

Her: Give me a break.

You: Think about all of the advantages that an older man can bring to you, and think about those boys that you usually date. Do you think that you could handle what an older man has to offer?

In both cases, you've turned the negative into a positive. It may take some work to get that shield down. After all, the age problem is always just an excuse she's using because she can't think of any better way to reject you—but if you stay focused on your questions and your final objective, that young soft thing will be yours.

After all, young girls are very impressionable.

The "Committed" Woman

*"HBs [honey bunnies] are never without a man.
They keep the one they have until they can
hook up something new. Then they skip off.
So, if you are waiting for an HB to become single,
you can forget it!"*

—Ray Parker (ASF)

Are you a sleazebag for picking up a woman in a "committed" relationship and having great sex with her? No. You're not forcing her to do anything. And the fact is, if the woman is hanging around, flirting with you, going on dates, or being overly friendly, she's practically begging you to do the right thing and make her toes curl.

In fact, women who are "taken" are even hornier and less picky than single women. They are less picky because they already have a man, so they're really only looking for some hot sex rather than a "perfect match." In other words, you don't need to impress her with your personality, just your ability to perform.

They are hornier because they love sex (that's why they're with a man in the first place), but they're obviously not getting the kind they need (that's why they're straying). In most cases the sex has become routine, and that leads to all kinds of problems: lack of interest on his part (especially when sports are on television), lack of foreplay, and falling asleep after he cums, but before she does. You would be surprised how many women are taken, but not satisfied. Which is why you're there to fulfill her desires and give her pleasure.

There are three signs that a woman is not only ready to step out on her man, but also ready to do it with you. Fortunately for you, the lessons have already been learned for you. So, take note of these three factors:

1. *She opens up to you about her relationship.* She may talk on and on about how wonderful it is. This is a classic case of "the lady doth protest too much." She is being so complimentary of the relationship because in reality it's not fulfilling her. More likely, she will admit to you all the ways the relationship isn't working, giving you the opportunity to fill those needs. Any time she wants to talk about her relationship, that's a good sign.

2. *She creates opportunities for the two of you to be together.* In some cases, she might be obvious enough to invite you somewhere (even if it is something as mundane as book reading or a lecture, remember that a woman inviting a man to anything is a positive sign). In other cases, it might be more subtle, like needing to come over to your house to "study" together or needing to borrow your car because hers is leaking oil. This is your opportunity to plug that leak! And don't be afraid of the fact that she wants to see you on "her time." She's in a relationship, she knows when the boyfriend is going to be around, so she controls when you get together. This isn't a bad thing; it's freaking paradise. You're getting sex, and you never even have to talk to the woman . . . except when she calls you to come over and have sex with her!

3. *She tells you about past cheating.* She may be "embarrassed" to tell you about her indiscretion and saying she would never do it again, but why would she bring it up if not to tell you that the door is open? If a woman tells you that she has cheated in the past, you should be planning to seduce this woman the next time you see her. Why? Because if a woman admits to past cheating, she is basically telling you that she plans to cheat again in the future . . . with you.

Remember: They wouldn't be in the game if they didn't want to play. Don't ever be intimidated by a boyfriend. No relationship is perfect. Every woman is looking for something or someone better. That someone is you.

I Have a Boyfriend

Don't ever, ever ask if she has a boyfriend! Maybe she does, maybe she doesn't—so what, who cares?

Maybe she has a boyfriend, but she wants to have a little fun. Your prompting about the *borefriend* will put her off the mood. She'll move on to another guy and get from him what she came looking for.

Maybe she has a borefriend but is curious about you and doesn't want his existence to scare you away. She might even dump him (at least for the night), if you're the guy you seem to be. Bringing up the borefriend just blows a hole in her plan, and loses you a fish that had already bitten on your hook.

Of course, there's always the chance she brings it up on her own, without your prompting. That's a bad sign, right? Not necessarily, my friend! She may have a borefriend but still be into you, which makes her feel guilty. If she tells you she has a borefriend, well, then, she's off the hook right? If you still want her and fuck her, it's not her fault because she told you and you didn't care, so she "had no choice" but to explore her dark side. Chick logic, yes, but the best kind of chick logic there is: the kind you can use.

Of course, in that scenario, she's going to be pretty flirty about the fact that she has a boyfriend, almost using it as a come-on. There will be other times when you can tell she's really loyal to her man and doesn't want to cheat on him—no matter how into you she is. This is a fine opportunity to do the gentlemanly thing and bail. After all, you're never going to care about her as much as some guy that's put in all that time and money to become her boyfriend.

On the other hand . . .

There is certainly a thrill in stealing a woman away from her borefriend, and no matter what she says, she may not feel anything serious about him. Many attractive women wear their boyfriends the way that they wear their purses—a boyfriend makes a nice accessory, letting the world know that the woman is sexual but not a slut. Like a purse, the woman may want to trade up when the season changes, and she may just be waiting to trade up to you. It's like a free pass to just go off on her and use every trick in the book. If you lose, well, she had a boyfriend so it's not your fault. If you win, well, just imagine the look on that chump's face when he finds out you're twice the man he'll ever be. Or even better, imagine the look on her face as you're taking her to places he's never been able to take her before.

So, if she throws the boyfriend blocker and you choose to stay in the pocket, here are a few techniques you can use to destroy that chump forever:

Ignore It

The first time she brings him up, just ignore it.

Her: Sorry, I have a boyfriend.
You: So, anyway, as I was saying . . .

There's a chance she may drop it forever, either because she was only trying to assuage her guilt or because you've given her a second to think about it and, on second thought, why let that AFC stand in the way of having a nice conversation with a confident alpha male? If she brings up the boyfriend again, move on to one of the following techniques.

The Humorous Approach

Maybe she was feeling guilty. Maybe she wanted to scare you away because she doesn't know you yet. Who cares? Just take it humorously, be light-hearted, and give her another chance.

Her: Sorry, I have a boyfriend
You (*laughing*)**:** Hey, I just met you and you're already telling me
  your problems!?

Even better, use a little humor to soften her up and then
place some doubt in her mind:

Her: Sorry, I have a boyfriend.
You: Great, if it makes you happy then bring him along! (*Pause.*)
  So, *does* he make you happy?

Downplay the Moment

Make it seem as if there's nothing incompatible about having
a boyfriend and talking (or even having sex) with you. Steer the
conversation away from sex, and away from the boyfriend, at
least until you break down her bitch shield and get to know her
better.

Her: Sorry, I have a boyfriend.
You: That's good, because I'm not really looking for a girlfriend.
  I'd rather find a girl I can talk to, really relate to . . .

Don't be smirky and sarcastic. This has to sound genuine.
Otherwise, she'll just think you're a dirtbag using a line to break
up a wonderful relationship—and yes, she will suddenly think
her relationship is wonderful once she senses your opportunism,
even if she didn't think so before.

Downplay the Relationship

A borefriend isn't a big deal. I mean, it's just a boyfriend,
not a lifelong commitment. Does she plan to never have sex with
anyone again?

Her: Sorry, I have a boyfriend.
You: It's pretty serious, I guess, since it's keeping you from meeting me. When's the wedding?

Or, if you want to lay it on a little thicker and make everything explicit, try this rap:

> It's really wonderful that you have a boyfriend. I can imagine how nice it would be to be able to share everything with someone else, to love and trust them completely, to know that they understand everything about you. You must be very happy. When are you planning to marry? It's obvious that you must be perfect together, that he satisfies every need you have. You must want to keep that happiness forever, and it's great to see two people ready to spend their lives together.

If she tells you the date, then you better hit the road or start working some of the more advanced boyfriend smashing techniques in the next section. If there's not a date, then obviously it's not that serious, right? Start eliciting her values and showing her you're the man of her dreams.

Those are quick hitters that shove the boyfriend question out of sight as soon as it comes up. After all, out of sight out of mind, right? Well, not always. In the next chapter, I'm going to give you an advanced strategy that hits the borefriend head on . . . and forces him out of the picture forever.

Alienate the Boyfriend

She says she has a boyfriend, but clearly he's not here. Where is he? Somewhere doing something stupid, because what he's done is leave you the perfect opening to start sowing seeds of doubt in her mind about the relationship, and about his fitness as a boyfriend in general.

Her: Sorry, I have a boyfriend.
You: And he's not here! I can't believe he'd let you out of his sights. Where is he?

If she doesn't have a good answer, like he's out of town on business or working late because he's a CEO, play the "he's cheating on you right now" angle. Whether they believe you or not is irrelevant (and they shouldn't, because obviously they know their borefriend much better than they know you, a total stranger). Your goal is to create an image in her mind of her bore-friend cheating on her. This alternative version of reality will eat away at her all night, causing her to doubt.

Never insult the boyfriend. Never say outright, "I bet he's cheating on you." In fact, you should be standing up for him and making "excuses" for his behavior. You're not trying to break up the relationship; you're on his side! Meanwhile, you keep asking leading questions about where he is, whether his friends like to pick up women (if he's out with the boys), and whether he likes to be away from her a lot. Ask her, "Is he out with the boys? Do his friends have as much luck picking up beautiful women as he does?" or "I always like to spend my evenings with beautiful women—whether I'm involved with them or not. I'm sure your boyfriend likes to do the same, so why isn't he here with you?" You're giving her compliments while sowing the seeds of doubt in her mind.

Now, work that seed of doubt by guiding the topic to cheating boyfriends. Tell her about a "friend" who was loyal to her boyfriend, then found out he was cheating on her and felt so stupid and used.

After all, a borefriend isn't forever, right? You can talk in general about wasting time and wasting your life, passing up great opportunities because of some promise you made to someone who isn't even there for you. Talk in general terms about all those little annoyances that come up in relationships, those day-to-day problems everyone experiences.

How will you know when you're making progress? When she starts mentioning things that are wrong with her boyfriend, even if she's still smiling and joking. She's not over him yet, but she's starting to open up to you. Even better, she's starting to focus on the negatives. If she gives you a specific complaint, ask her some follow-up questions so that she has to really think about all the negative implications.

Finally, it's time to talk about ex-boyfriends. Did they treat her the same way? Is there possibly something wrong with her? If you can get her to start talking about one ex-boyfriend in particular, you will have done two very important things. First, she's thinking about a man other than her man. Second, she's realizing that boyfriends are temporary things, and that the loyalty she feels now is just another version of a loyalty she felt in the past . . . and eventually left behind.

If the ex she chooses to talk about was a jerk, a cheater, or an AFC, focus on how wrong she was about him when they were going out and how much better she felt after she'd left him. The implication: leaving a boyfriend is a positive.

If the ex she chooses to talk about was a great guy (and surprisingly most women like to talk about hot and heavy ex-relationships), coax her along with memories of how passionate their love-making was and how horny he used to make her. Chances are, her current boyfriend will pale in comparison. Maybe she felt the same way about him once, but in all long-term relationships that passionate intensity fades. And, of course, you always want what you can't have—in this case, the ex-boyfriend.

In fact, she's getting horny right now just thinking about him, so start giving her a little kino . . . shoulder massage, back rub, hold her from behind, stuff she doesn't get every day from her absentee lover. She's going to want to release that pent up passion somewhere, and believe me, she's going to want to release it with you!

Girls' Night Out

Here's a great boyfriend-smashing exchange that grew out of a classic in *Sweep Women off Their Feet and into Your Bed*. This one takes place on a girls' night out when a bunch of female friends leave their men to hang out together like old times. This is one of the most challenging (but rewarding) ways to meet a woman. In this case, the track is even harder because the woman is ready and willing to stand up for her man . . . at least for a little while.

You: It's great that you can go out and have such fun with your girlfriends. Do you ever miss your boyfriend when you hear a slow dance? Don't you want to feel his kiss, his hands on you, on the dancefloor, rather than sitting out like a wallflower?

Her: We need some time to be apart with our own friends, too. He respects my independence.

You: Wow, it's great to be with a man that respects your independence. Do you think that he ever thinks about the men that you might meet out there, the guys that will want to dance with you or buy you a drink?

Her: He knows I'm not interested in those guys.

You: Does he like you to go out without him often? It's great that you have a wonderful boyfriend, but it makes me think a little, too. Does he stay home when you're out? Does he go out with the boys when you're out with the girls?

Her: Sometimes he does—I'm out too.

You: Yes, that's right. You're out with the girls. Are all his friends guys, or does he have a night out with girls too? Do the guys try to pick up women? I'm sure he wouldn't do that, but it makes you wonder—if they're doing it, what is he doing?

Don't get me wrong, you seem to have a great relationship. It's just that if I had a wonderful girl like you, I'd want to be with her as much as I could. I can't see how he can stand not to spend every minute looking into your eyes, rubbing your arm gently, whispering softly to you. He must be a great guy, though, the kind that surprises you with weekends in Vermont and little gifts under your pillow when you least expect it. He would have to be, because you seem like the kind of woman who would want and deserve that.

He must be that kind of guy. I know he'd never take you for granted, because you could have any guy you wanted, and he would know that. Any man would look at you and see that you deserve everything. I bet he's sitting at home right now, waiting for you to call. He must be, or he couldn't hold on to you."

If she goes to the phone at any point during the evening, that's a good sign. She's looking for reassurance that he's home. Even if he is home, there's a good chance they'll fight. After all, you've planted and fertilized those seeds of doubt. If they have even the smallest argument, you have a chance. Start treating her like she would want her boyfriend to treat her, and work on those desires for romance.

PART

4

Closing the Deal

CHAPTER 12

The Close

Entering the Final Phase

Closing is the final phase of a seduction: the time when you move from pick up to hook up. You've approached the girl, you've gotten to know her, you've become the man she wants you to be. Now, it's time to maneuver her into your arms.

Never say, "Well, it was great to meet you. Bye now." What have you gained from that? The conversation is useless unless you extract something from the girl—her phone number, a promise for a new meeting, a kiss. If your timing is right, you should get all three.

So how do you know when to initiate the close? As a general rule, you should close her at a high point in the conversation after she gives you three signs of interest.

What are the signs of interest, again? They're listed on page 155, but here's a reminder of a few of the most powerful signs a woman can give you. And remember, as always, it's not what she says—it's all in the body language.

The Most Important Signs of Interest

- She holds your eye contact for a second, then looks down and away.
- She smiles or laughs in response to something you've said.
- She "opens up" to you by turning her body toward you and putting her arms to her side.
- She mirrors your body language.
- She caresses or rubs herself, or runs her hand through her hair. This is not to be confused with pinching or gripping herself, which is a sign she wants you to leave her alone and never come back.
- She touches you, especially as a response to kino. If she responds to your kino by upping the ante—for instance, if you touch her on the hand and she rubs your arms—move directly to the close.

Sex Talk

I'll talk about the actual act of closing in a later section, but first I want to touch on one of the most important elements of any seduction situation: sex talk.

Unless you're using GM style, you should never start a conversation with sex talk or sexual innuendos. Don't misunderstand me: the emphasis is on the word *start*. If you start an encounter with sexual banter, chances are you'll never get the opportunity to try anything else. Unless you're using the GM technique to harvest girls who are blatantly and shamelessly interested in nothing but sex, don't mix it in with your repertoire . . . until you think she's interested in you.

Establish rapport with the girl. Understand her values and echo them back to her. Notice her body language becoming more friendly and open. Now move on to sexual talk. Quote her a sexual situation (for instance, "My friend Kate once told me about getting a quick fuck from a guy she hardly knew") and watch her reaction. Be sensitive, but be bold. You're pushing the envelope here in an attempt to make her drop her inhibitions. That's why quoting is so effective. You can safely talk about graphic sex and she can safely get horny because, after all, you're not talking about each other.

Most women will slightly recoil when you drop sex into the conversation for the first time. This is simply their natural "gut" reaction, and not a reflection of their true feelings. If you feel confident you're in the zone (in other words, she's been giving you the signs), don't back off. Pursue the topic with no apologies, and she will usually spring back to a very positive reaction. This isn't true of all cases, but if you've calibrated the girl correctly, you should be able to see whether she's truly appalled by your dirty talk, or merely hesitant but intrigued.

Sex talk is the perfect bridge from conversation to closing because it changes the entire dynamic of the relationship. Once you bring up sex, she will immediately be forced to think about having sex with you. If she finds this a pleasant or intriguing idea, she will echo the sex talk back to you. Once you're engaged in sexual banter, even of the joking type, you are in. This girl is yours. Move on to closing immediately.

But be warned: sexual banter does not mean she wants to have sex with you. It just means she is contemplating the idea and interested in pursuing it further, for instance over a cup of coffee or in a phone conversation. There's still work to do, but from this point on, it's your game to lose.

Sexual Talk Plus

Sexual talk can also lead to an even better topic of conversation: sexual fantasies and kinks. The key is to calibrate the girl and, hopefully, understand what she really wants in a man. Some women—and thank God for this!—just want some really hot, passionate sex. Maybe she already has a boyfriend who's not fulfilling her; maybe she's a bad girl; maybe she's just in a horny mood and wants to do something wild just once in her life. The reason doesn't matter: it's your follow-up that counts.

The Anti–Sex Talk Position

I'm a big fan of sex talk, but even I will admit that sometimes being a little too forward can cause a caught fish to wriggle off your hook. You never truly know how a girl is going to react when you bring up sex talk. If she's not ready to think about having sex with you, then she could drop kick you out of her life right there.

That's why some PUAs swear off sex talk entirely. No sex comments. No sex jokes. No innuendo. Instead, they use kino to ratchet up the sexual tension. They touch her. If she's responding to Kino, keep going further. This way, she can respond to your sexual advance without having to hear or say anything that might be off-putting to her in a public situation. Once you're kissing and getting into it, it's time to close and walk away. Remember, PUAs always leave women wanting more.

You've started the sexual talk by quoting something that happened to a "friend" and she's responded positively. You could move on to closing, but you've got a feeling about this girl. So, drop her a fantasy. Mention how much your friend loves being in a purely sexual relationship because she's free to do anything she wants without fear of being judged by her lover.

Watch the woman's reaction. Did that idea dampen her spirits, or did she seem to respond positively to the suggestion? If she smiles or touches you at the thought, mention a couple you know where the woman isn't getting what she wants but is afraid to ask for it. In a purely physical relationship, this would never happen because it's all about exploring fantasies and acting out on them.

If she agrees with you, she will immediately respond positively. You are in! This woman is looking for a great fuck, no strings attached. You may even be talking her into that once-in-a-lifetime walk on the wild side! Start exploring specific ideas, such as different sexual positions, public sex, threesomes. Don't go overboard with your personal fantasies. Listen carefully to what *her* deepest desires are and play into them. If everything clicks, after about five minutes she will practically want to rape you. This is one of those times when you should skip closing and head straight home.

Make a Timely Exit

Always remember that the close is what you came for. All that other stuff (and fluff) was just the bridge to get you to this point. In other words, you should always try to get to the close as quickly as possible!

If you can close the girl after the approach, by all means do so. In some cases, there is no need to elicit values at all. In others, such as on the street, in a coffee shop, or someplace else where she's not expecting an advance, there's no time or opportunity to start an involved conversation. In these cases, she doesn't have to give you the signs. Don't worry. If you stop her on the street, and she actually smiles and talks to you, that's all you need. Use the element of surprise—and the flattery implicit in your advance—to move directly to the close.

Lots of guys (loser AFCs, of course) make the fatal mistake of not closing a woman quickly when the opportunity arises. They think, "As long as the conversation is going well, I should just keep at it. If I move too fast, she'll just think I'm a horndog. The more time I spend with her, after all, the better!" This is absolutely, positively false. If you're demonstrating personality and making her laugh, end the conversation.

That's right, the more she likes you, the sooner you should leave. Why? Because no matter how interesting you are, you're eventually going to run out of things to say. It's better to leave before that happens, when you seem endlessly fascinating, than after that inevitable lull in the conversation. By leaving first, and on a high note, there's no chance that she's going to think you're

Diane in New York City describes her feelings when she's talking with a man who stays with her after his friends leave:
"There's suddenly a lot of pressure on. He should always
leave with his friends. He can simply say he doesn't want to
ditch them, then ask if he can call me. He comes off like a
good pal and not just someone on the make."

pestering her out of desperation. In fact, she's going to feel, at
least unconsciously, that she wants you more than you want her.

So you just leave, even if she's the best thing going? Yes, you
always leave, *especially* if she's the best thing going. And even if
you have nowhere else to go. Use any excuse: you need to get
back to your friends, you have an errand to run, you have an
appointment. Women like men who are busy. It makes it seem like
you have a life. Even walking out the door and strolling around
the neighborhood for fifteen minutes is a better option than lin-
gering in a great conversation, provided you get her number.

The last thing you want to do with a woman, after all, is talk
yourself out of topics. Always remain mysterious; always just
give her a taste and leave her wanting more; that's the PUA way.

Proceeding Instead of Closing

Although the closing is what you came for, sometimes you don't
have to close. If you're both having a wonderful time, and things
are going well, why would you literally want to "close" out a
good thing? To leave her wanting more? To work some magic
over the phone and build up anticipation, connection, and attraction? Sounds good, but why not just proceed straight to the
action?

Well, as I discussed before, there are actually a million reasons why you shouldn't stay with a seduction just because it's
going well: she might begin to think you're pestering her; the

conversation might lag; you might start to look desperate; you might talk yourself out and have nothing for later.

Sometimes, however, it's clear there's a chance things could happen right now. If you're not busy, and she appears ready to reschedule her day for you, then why not give it a shot? This is called proceeding. It's not recommended, but it can work wonders in the right circumstances.

The key to proceeding is to get you to go on a "date" with her right there. In other words, suggest a change of venue where the two of you can get more comfortable. A cup of coffee is ideal for the middle of the day, but even just a nice walk will do. The key is simply to get her out of the current environment, and into a place where you and she can be alone together. Even if that place is crowded with strangers, it doesn't matter, because none of these new people know you just picked her up. They probably think you've known each other for months. This isn't important for you, but it's probably very important for her.

Now that you've got her out on a "date," flip to the next section and find out how to move from coffee and tea to me (or in this case—you).

The Number Close

Closing isn't about having sex right there, or even taking the woman home. Most of the time, seduction just doesn't work that way. The object of every seduction situation is to get her phone number and a promise to meet again. If she'd rather come home with you right now, well, I won't argue with that, but never expect that outcome. You'll only go home disappointed.

Every time you leave a woman, you must close her. Even if you are planning to come back and talk to her in fifteen minutes (after that brisk walk around the block that makes you look busy), you must extract a phone number and a promise to meet again before you step aside. What if she suddenly has to leave? What if you can't find her again? Never take that risk; get that number. The simplest way to do this is to simply ask.

You: I don't mean to be direct, but what's your phone number?

Or, even better:

You: Give me your phone number (*handing her a pen and something to write on*).

Or best of all:

You: I have an intuition . . . and I don't know if you can imagine this as I describe it . . . that when we get a chance to talk without time pressures and interruptions . . . we'll really enjoy each other's company . . . and I'm wondering if there's a number where you feel comfortable having me call you?

After all, the direct approach is always the best, right? Wrong. In the case of the Number Close, the direct approach is not the way to go. Your object is to get her number, but make it seem like it's *her* idea to give it to you. This way you're leaving her with the thought, "I gave him my number . . . I must like him" as opposed to the standard thought, "He asked for my number . . . he must like me." In the first situation, she's the one with the desire so you've got the power; in the second, you're just another chump trying to pick her up. If she's model beautiful, or even good-looking enough to be popular (and why would you try to pick up anyone else?), then you just wimped yourself out of ever seeing her again.

Instead of the above, say something like, "So . . . what steps would we have to take in order to make sure we talk again?" You've implied that you'd like her number, but she's actually going to be the one to suggest giving it to you. Does this trick make a difference? You better believe it does.

But there's an even better way to close a girl you've just had a great conversation with. Remember, you're leaving at a high point, with her laughing and loving your company. You've given her a taste, and hopefully she wants more. So, suddenly realize that you have to leave (look at your watch, check the time with her, etc.), and tell her you'd love to get together again.

Suggest something specific—and preferably something she's recently told you she likes! But no dates, of course. That's the AFC way. Take her for coffee near her office instead of dinner. Go rollerblading instead of to the movies.

If you approach the situation this way, she will probably offer you her number. If not, use one of these lines to coax it out of her:

You: So . . . what steps should we take to make sure we talk again?

Or:

You: Great. I'll call you tomorrow.
Her: But you don't have my number!
You: Oh, that's right (*and pull out a pen*).

Or:

You: I can't wait to go bicycling together. (*She nods.*) But for this to happen you have to ask me a question.
Her: Can I have your number?
You: Wow, you come on strong! Are you always this bold?
Her: I know what I want.
You (*acting impressed*)**:** All right, how about we trade numbers, then?

Or simply tell the woman you just realize that you're late for an appointment. You've had a great time, and you really enjoyed meeting her, and then walk away. Walk for about twenty paces, stop and stand still (in case she's watching you and wondering why you didn't ask her out), then turn around and come back to the table. Smile and say, "You know what? If we ever want to do this again, laugh and have a good time, we need to know how to get a hold of each other, because if we didn't get together again we'd really be missing out on some intriguing conversations, some laughs, having a good time. So what do you figure we should do about that?"

> The best thing he can do is try to make a date off of our common interests. If we were talking about golf, "We should go to the driving range sometime," is a great thing to say. It's not like the pressure of a date . . . If I want to see you, I'll pick up on your invite.
>
> —Phoebe, Westport, Connecticut

In all these instances, the answer the girl is supposed to give is obvious. But what if she doesn't respond like she should? That's when you go right back up to the top of this section and ask her directly for her phone number. It's the AFC way to go, but it's definitely better than no number at all.

Closing the Number Close

This is extremely important: once you get her number, never just tell her, "Great, I'll call you some time," or "I'll be calling you soon." Always give her a specific time that you are going to call. Say, "Great. I'll call you tomorrow around 5:00. Is that a good time for you?"

If possible (and why wouldn't it be, it's just a phone call), always set up the call for the next day. Playing hard to get is for suckers. You want her to know you're interested in her, and you want to show that interest by calling her as soon as possible. Don't worry, this doesn't come across as desperate. It just shows you're a man who knows what he wants and isn't afraid to go after it.

And always leave her with a suggestion that romance is in the future. Clifford (of *Clifford's Seduction Newsletter*) suggests the direct approach. When exchanging phone numbers, he likes to say, "Is our relationship going to be romantic? Because I like romance." I prefer the more subtle approach of suggesting that I hope the activity (rollerblading, coffee, etc.) leads to more interesting things. You've planted the idea, but you haven't come on too strong or needy.

And finally, I always try to use a few lines to soften her up for the phone call.

You: When I call you, I don't want you to answer, "Huh? Who? Ah . . . it's you . . . so how's it goin'?" I want you to act really enthusiastic and happy, like, "Oh, you called! God, I'm so glad." Okay? Is it a deal?

Say it as if you're joking (kind of), with a big smile. This ends the exchange on a light, friendly, and positive note—and that almost automatically kick-starts the phone call from the same place. In fact, many girls will repeat the answer I suggested back to me. They're joking, but those positive qualities are still on their minds.

Troubleshooting the Number Close

You've structured an opportunity for her to offer her phone number. That didn't work, so you asked for her phone number. That didn't work either. No problem, because you're not dead yet. You just need to understand why she she's being so reluctant, and then go from there.

If She Says No to Your Request

If she seems reluctant to give you her phone number, it may just be that she is simply overwhelmed by your request—especially if you rushed things and tried to go straight from the approach to the close. Whatever you do, don't ask for the number again or try to pester her into giving it to you. This only makes you look desperate, and makes her more overwhelmed and suspicious of your motives. Remain polite and safe, like it's no big deal that she didn't trust you with this information.

But remember that persistence pays! So stay in there and keep the conversation going (even if you used the appointment excuse, you can squeeze out another five minutes). You're back into eliciting values mode now, so you've given yourself another chance to win her and close her properly.

If you've learned where she works during the conversation, and you still want to get with her, wait three days and then call her office. She'll probably act like she doesn't remember you, but don't let that put you off. If she asks how you tracked her down in an intrigued voice (as opposed to the angry, "I'm going to turn you in as a stalker" voice), ask her out for some coffee near her office. If she's angry, you're probably best to leave her alone and consider this a learning experience. After all, if there's one thing you've learned so far, it's that there are plenty of beautiful women waiting for you. You don't want to seem obsessed or angry with just one, especially one as angry and distrustful as her.

If She Asks for Your Number Instead

Don't give your phone number to her. Many women are collectors—they like to get phone numbers, but they have no intention of using them. Some even have a little competition with their friends to see who can get the most numbers in a week or month. Is she looking at you as just another sucker for her unused Rolodex, or is she just uncomfortable giving out her number to a virtual stranger?

It doesn't matter, because either way you should accuse her of being a "naughty girl playing a naughty girl game to collect numbers and impress her friends." If she is just playing, you've showed her that you're not just another chump—and hopefully earned her respect. Chances are, though, that she'll deny she's playing a game and try to convince you she's not that kind of girl. Tell her there's one way to convince you: by giving you her number.

Or you can go with the "honest" reply, something along the lines of, "I keep a very hectic schedule. If you call me, you'll probably end up developing a long lasting and fulfilling relationship with my answering machine. I'm in and out a lot. However, with your number I could call you when I'm able to talk."

If she says that she's busy as well, tell her that you can double your odds of reaching each other if both of you have each other's numbers.

The Kiss Close

You should always follow up the Number Close with an attempt to kiss her. Often, you will be able to tell from her body language that she is ready and waiting for the good-bye kiss. She will let you touch her without resistance and touch you in return; she will wet her lips or look at your lips; she will move in closer to you. These are subconscious signals of her desire on her part. Read them and take advantage of them.

Do not expect her to come right out and ask for a kiss. We all wish it were that easy, but this is just not the female style. *It's your duty to make the move*, so lean in and give her the kiss that will keep her wanting more. If you can, and she seems receptive, you can even try to give her an openmouthed kiss. If her body language is a little more closed, however, stick to a close-mouthed kiss, but try to have it last a few seconds.

But what if things aren't so clear? What if the signals are mixed, or she seems reluctant to give you her phone number? Or the conversation just didn't go that well? Now is not the time to wimp out! The dumbest thing you can do is leave without finding out whether she would have kissed you or not. In this case, it's better to fail than to never try.

Of course, you have to be smart about the situation. For instance, if she's with her family, don't try the kiss close. Even if she wants to kiss you, the situation is awkward—especially if you've just met. The same can sometimes be true if her friends are standing right there. That's why it's always best to extract her from the group before trying to close.

In all other cases, however, you *must* go for the Kiss Close. Don't ask, "Can I kiss you?" That old line indicates supplicating AFC tendencies, and it puts her on a pedestal from which its too easy to reject you. Why give her the opportunity?

Chump File: Kissing Gimmicks

Closing isn't difficult if you've done your work (eliciting values, creating rapport), but some guys still want to take a shortcut and use a gimmick. The most common is the "kiss argument." This involves picking up on some characteristic the girl has dropped to you in conversation—her hometown, her job, her hobby—and insisting that women from that place or working that kind of job don't know how to kiss right. They'll usually argue, at which point you say, "Well, let's find out" and give her the long luscious action.

But, let me play devil's advocate for a moment and point out that:

1. Most women will see through this trick, and . . .
2. You better have kino with the girl and make sure she's into you before trying this maneuver, otherwise you're going to get bitch slapped, and . . .
3. If you have kino and she likes you and you're a decent pick-up artist, you will be making out with her soon anyway. In other words, this gimmick is just a shortcut. Is it really worth it to trick the girl into a kiss, when you could make her horny for it in less than five minutes? I don't think so.

Still, if you wish to take this approach, here's another suggestion. SirMoby (ASF) asks women if they like ice cream. The women usually answer yes, and ask him why he asks. SirMoby says, "I explain that women that don't like ice cream usually kiss with their mouths closed . . . and seem to have no passion . . . I usually get an open mouth kiss in a few minutes, and they also start telling me about their passions."

Instead, if things are unclear, say to her, "Would you like to kiss me?" If the response is anything but a direct "No!" then go for the kiss.

Don't expect a "yes" to this question. It's just too hard for some women to be that forward with a man (but if she is, you can safely assume you would get the same answer to the question, "Would you like to make love to me all night?"). The lack of an outright refusal—such as silence or an "I don't know"—usually means that the woman wants to kiss you, but she's holding back because of the social or personal implications. So you should say, "Let's find out" and go directly for the best kiss she's ever had. Trust me, she'll like it.

If the reply is a blatant "no," you better neg her quickly to get back your control of the situation. Say something like, "Gee, you sure wrecked a great moment. I bet your previous boyfriends must have hated that about you." Are you risking the fact that she won't pick up your call? Yes. But more likely, she'll re-evaluate her position and be ready to kiss you next time around.

Ejecting

> "I don't need to win all the time. I size up a woman's potential and either go for it or move on and cut my losses fast. Sometimes the best choice is just to say 'adios' and move on. When you realize you don't have to win (or close) all the time, then it takes the pressure off and you become much more relaxed. Ironically, and paradoxically, this almost always leads to your winning far more often than you ever imagined possible!"
>
> —Ross Jeffries (www.seduction.com)

Remember, no individual woman is all-important! There are always more fish in the sea, and if this one isn't working out for any reason, it's your prerogative to cast your net elsewhere.

Maybe she hasn't risen to meet your high standards. Or maybe, for whatever reason, she isn't interested. Hey, it happens—all the time. If you are getting none of the signals of interest in a reasonable amount of time (five minutes) with a reasonable amount of effort (at least three attempts to move on to eliciting values) to demonstrate value and entertain her, then *simply move on*.

So many uninitiated chumps just linger on forever in hopes of getting the girl interested, maybe, somehow, at some point . . . which leaves the bored and frustrated woman no option but to eject him herself. This is not good for your image or your psyche.

If, however, you know when to cut your losses and move on, you can end the conversation on a high note (leaving an opening for future interaction), show that you're not desperate or overeager (enhancing your image for future interaction), and spend your precious time interacting with women who appreciate you. You offered her a hot opportunity, and she failed to grasp it. You have no need to push it—you know your game is golden, so just eject and move on.

Persistence pays, but knowing when to "hold them, and when to fold them," as old Kenny Rogers sang, is the sign of a professional pick-up artist (and gambler). She doesn't want what you're offering? Tell her, "The night is young, and perhaps I'll see you again. It was a pleasure meeting you."

The Specialty Close: Our World

The Our World routine is an advanced technique that, according to rumor, is a sure way to get an interested but hesitant girl over the hump.

Our World constructs an imaginary world for both you and the girl, where the two of you can feel happy, comfortable, relaxed, and free to do anything you wish, irrespective of the rules and norms of society or the attitudes of other people. This is because, quite simply, you are now in a different world, a world without any outside influences, a world where normal rules don't apply, a world for just the two of you. You are in "our world."

Our World is the perfect closer because the desired outcome is for the girl to agree on ending up at your place the next time you two meet (it also works very well when arranging a "date" over the phone). It's also ideal for overcoming any objections she may express, because in "our world," you are both free from the ordinary rules and conventions that hold people down and keep us from enjoying life to the fullest. "Our world" is an ideal world, especially for love.

But you can't build her ideal world until you know exactly what it needs to be like. So, as in all seduction encounters, you have to find out her values, her principles, and her possible objections to ending up at your place.

After you've done enough value-eliciting and know her possible objections (she might have a boyfriend or be afraid of social labeling, etc.), you can start building the perfect world for the two of you, which represents all that she values, circumvents everything she objects to, but most importantly—and this is what you are striving for—is free of any usual social restrictions and objections to sharing, loving, touching, and feeling wonderful in each other's company (you know where this list is headed).

The following example is modified from an original post from Maniac High, in which he describes the technique of a fellow successful PUA.

> The first thing to do is elicit values and find her interests as quickly as you can, then use those interests to bring in romance. If she's interested in travel, ask her if she had a boyfriend who traveled, and if she liked snowboarding, ask her if she had a boyfriend who snowboarded. Whatever her interests are, move onto the man as quickly as you can. Then, start asking what that boyfriend was like. If she didn't have a boyfriend who shared those interests, ask her if she ever had a boyfriend that shared any of her interests, then ask what he was like. What you're trying to do is

switch the talk to romance, to men, to her views of life, and the nature of people. You have to make sure she's following you, though, and isn't bored by the conversation. If she's moving along with you, continue; if not, switch themes.

If the conversation is going well, you continue talking about what human nature is like and what all people want—feeling closeness to other people, support and unconditional love, warmth, and companionship. Find out what matters to her in these things, and how she feels restricted (you should already have picked up on some of these things when you elicited values).

At this point, introduce the idea of "our world," a world where the rules of society don't have to apply and where you can get all of those things people want—you can hug and feel close, cuddle and feel supported, be near someone and feel warmth and companionship. She should feel secure and free to feel these things, because they take place in "our world," away from the pressures of society.

At this point, she should be feeling great about you, so you won't scare her off if you suggest that she come over to your place sometime so that the two of you can create "our world." Tell her how you can cuddle, hug, and make each other feel warm and safe—and tell her that being together doesn't mean just sex. (Remember, you're trying to give her a feeling of safety and security.) You might say, "When you're close to someone, feeling really warm and secure in their touch, sex seems like a recognition of those wonderful feelings that you give each other." At this point, you can usually get a woman to agree to set a date with you.

You aren't done yet, though. She may feel excited to come over, and she may not. And even if she feels comfortable with you at the moment, there's no guarantee that she won't get scared at the last minute and run away. She'll feel much more comfortable and secure if you let her know what to expect in advance. To give her that feeling of comfort and security, describe in detail what your next meeting will be like. Not only should doing this make her more comfortable, it will help build the anticipation in her mind. Use beautiful, wonderful, uplifting, and positive terms to describe the meeting. Add some details—they will help get her imagination going.

Here's an example of what you might say: "You'll arrive at my building just as the sun is setting. There's a beautiful, soft light over everything. When I open the door, you'll notice that it's warm inside. I give you a gentle kiss, and I'll take your hand and lead you to the living room. You'll notice that the light is soft and gentle, and there's calm music playing. Everything will be safe and secure. I'll sit next to you on the sofa, taking your hand in mine. We can sit there comfortably together and talk—maybe cuddle together if you want, it's up to you. We'll be alone and safe in 'our world,' where we can do as much or as little as we want . . ."

Now that you've set the script in her mind, it's time to end the encounter. When the day arrives, do everything that you can to make it exactly as you promised—including the lighting and the music.

When you meet her, hug her and welcome her to "our world." Give her a little kiss, just like you've said. Your touch should warm her up to what will happen inside.

Lead her inside and sit down. Talk to her about how warm and comfortable a hug would feel, then give her a hug. Give her another kiss—after all, you've started outside, so she shouldn't mind. A few gentle rubs on the arm or back, then some more kissing, then a gentle touch on the breast . . . I think that you can take it from here.

According to Maniac, this technique works for his friend every time, and "he could lay a girl about twenty minutes" after they walked in the door. Sound too good to be true? Try it yourself and find out!

CHAPTER **13**

The "Date"

The Phone Call

There's no breaking the golden rule: call her when you said you were going to call her—the very next day after meeting her. And remember what this phone call is about: setting up a time to meet her again.

The PUA community is divided over the power of the phone as a seduction tool. Some guys think it's a powerful way to seduce women because the women are in the privacy of their own homes, away from prying eyes (including yours) so they can open up and be more responsive to your questions and suggestions. Some guys claim they can even make women orgasm just through the power of their voice. A good trick, sure, but I'd rather have her orgasm with me!

Most seducers agree with me that the phone conversation is the kiss of death. You want to do your seduction in person, not from across town, so always get right to the point with your follow-up phone call. The best way to do this is to tell her you're very busy and only have a minute to talk, but you don't want to miss the opportunity to be with her again. Being "busy" is one of the great tools of a PUA, as you'll learn in the next section, so it's

> If she's unsure, you can always use patterning over the phone, as in this example from Ross Jeffries (www.seduction.com), to be used after a little fluff talk but before the invite: "In fact, I don't know if you can recognize that with each little giggle . . . with each breath you take . . . with each beat of your heart . . . you're growing more intrigued, but anyway . . . just setting aside whatever pictures just keep popping into your mind when I say that . . ."

important to establish the fact that you're a busy and important person early on.

Always suggest a place to meet that is: (1) convenient for both of you, (2) casual, and (3) something she finds interesting. Don't suggest coffee if she's a Mormon; don't suggest a walk in the park if she's having a hay fever attack.

While the phone call should be brief and to the point, keep the techniques that you've learned so far—such as eliciting values—in mind. Now, I'll admit, it's a little more difficult to elicit values over the phone than in person, especially for a beginner. That's why you need to exploit the advantage the phone gives you: she can't see what you're doing. Before you call, feel free to write down a few seductive lines of questioning and conversation topics, then simply consult the list if the need arises. Write down her trance words and values, too. Now it's as easy as reading those words and values back to her. Just make sure your delivery is natural; reading from a script has never impressed an intelligent woman (and only a few dumb ones).

Once you've worked out the arrangements, get the hell off the phone! There's no reason this phone call should take more than a minute—and anything over five minutes is far too long. Make it sweet. Make it simple. And save your energy for what counts—making sure the meeting is right.

The Work Number

Sometimes you will have acquired a beautiful woman's phone number through non-seduction means, such as on a business or sales call. Is it okay to exploit this opportunity for sexual purposes? As long as it's not going to get you fired, you bet it is! Following up a fluke phone number is a bit different than calling a woman you've already closed, so try this approach, based on one developed by Johnny Shack:

After you introduce yourself tell her that something about her drew you to her, and you felt that you had to call her. When she replies, tell her that you're an emotional person, and you don't like to hold back your feelings. Tell her that you knew you'd be tossing and turning all night if you didn't call her. Remember to keep it light, and say this in a humorous way—you're not a supplicating AFC. A woman shouldn't be sure if you are serious or you are joking. Finally, tell her that you think the two of you should follow up and get together to know each other better—maybe over coffee or for a walk in the park. Recommend a day and time, then, when you get an answer, get off the phone as quickly as you can. She'll be intrigued, wondering how serious you are about her, and you'll have your foot in the door.

Asking for a . . . Date?

No, you're not going to ask for a date. First of all, PUAs don't ask, they offer opportunities. And secondly, movies, museums, and dinners out are for girls that have already convinced you they mean business in the only credible fashion possible—by having done the fun (and I don't mean playing Monopoly).

Instead, you are going to suggest a get-together, preferably somewhere where the two of you can talk (and touch) and get to

Chump File: Playing the Dating Game

Here's a recent anonymous internet post that I just couldn't resist commenting on in this book. The writer thinks he's playing it PUA cool, but he's really just an AFC in wolf's clothing.

Make sure you're the one who ends the date, not her. Let's say you are eating in a restaurant after having seen a movie . . . [*She better be paying her way, chump, because you don't pay until she's let you play—all the way home.*] . . . you need to maintain control over the evening, not allow it to continue to the point when she decides she wants to go home. [*Are you even eliciting values? Getting kino? Moving on to sex talk? Or are you just fluff talking her all night?*] You should announce that it's getting late and it's time to go while the conversation is still going well, and the date is still at a high point. [*Right advice, pal, but wrong setting. By the time you're on a date like this, she should have already gone home with you*] Let her know that you had a good time . . . [*What a lie, because your goal wasn't to stuff your stomach and gape at a movie, it was to make her hornier than she's ever been, and give her the orgasm of her life*] . . . and that you would enjoy seeing her again some time. She won't be expecting this . . . [*It surprises me that you're not even going to kiss close, fool.*] . . . because she's used to guys who hang on for as long as possible, as though that would somehow magically result in sex. [*Well, duh, that will never work, but you've got to try to get action every time you're out with a woman or you're never going to succeed.*] She will let you know if sex is in the cards. [*Don't leave it up to her! It's* your *job to make her crazy for it.*] So, if she hasn't given you these signals . . . [*You haven't tried hard enough, and you've wasted a lot of time and money.*] . . . declare the date over at a high point. [*There*

> *is no high point if she isn't giving you signals. If she isn't responding, you should have ejected her a long time ago.*] You won't seem like all the other guys she's dated. [*Yes, you will. They didn't get any, and neither did you.*] You'll seem like a catch who isn't so easy to get. [*Or that you're a chump and a wimp like all the other guys.*]

know each other uninterrupted. You need to make it perfectly clear that this is not a "date" without saying so directly to the girl. You do this by always suggesting a meeting in the middle of the week. The weekend, especially at night, always seems like a date, no matter how casual you try to make the get-together. And by asking her out for the weekend, you're sending all kinds of wrong messages: that you don't have anything to do on the weekend already; that you're arranging your schedule around her; that she's the only woman you have going.

The odds are also higher she'll be available on a weekday, creating a feeling of synchronicity and getting her into the habit of saying yes. It reinforces the relaxed, no-pressure "just a get-together" message you're trying to send, overcoming any feelings she may have that you're coming on too strong. And you've turned a boring Wednesday into an exciting meeting with a mysterious man. Those good vibes will definitely carry over into the rest of the evening.

The Power of Suggestion

Now that you know that the "date" in "asking for a date" is not a date at all, it's time to tackle that other problem word: asking. PUAs never ask a woman for *anything*. Instead, you create opportunities, just like you created an opportunity for her to ask for your phone number before asking for hers.

So never take the supplicating, AFC way out by asking, "So, do you want to go out with me sometime?" or "Could we please get together, please, please, please!" You're putting her on a pedestal and groveling at her feet. You're giving her every reason and opportunity to kick you right out of her life. And, even if she does accept your pathetic invitation, you've still lost control of the relationship, and you're probably never going to get it back.

Besides, if you ask her out and she automatically responds "no," she won't even give you another thought. But if you suggest a casual meeting and offer a time and place, she'll first have to think about what she's doing at that time and whether she likes that place. If it turns out she's busy (which she may well be), she is much more likely to offer another time or another place. You've made her think about meeting you, and that's always a good thing.

So, always say, "We should meet. This place on this day at this time sounds great for me. Are you free?"

If you sense some hesitation ("Maybe some other time.") or outright hostility ("Sorry, my schedule is full until next year."), you'll need to pull out your big guns. Start by negging, then continue on to eliciting values. Even if she was trying to blow you off before, she'll usually feel guilty enough to talk to you, so this is your chance to win her back PUA-style. Let her know she has wasted your time. Find out why she is hesitating. Pace her reality so that she sees how rude and irrational it would be to refuse to hang out with you after you have developed a connection.

You Probably Ask Girls Out All the Time . . .

If she says this, don't lie. This isn't a bad thing for her to know. In fact, some PUAs intentionally drop into their suggestion of a meeting the fact that meeting women isn't new to them. They'll say something like:

> I've taken women to some of the nicest restaurants and theatres in town, and it's been great. But I've also been with women when all we did was drink coffee, and I've liked that even more. It all depends on whether you need the scenery for support . . . and I'm betting we don't. So let's just take this casual and get a coffee tomorrow.

This accomplishes a number of things. It lets her know that you get around and that lots of other women find you desirable. It shows her that meeting a woman for coffee isn't a big deal for you, which takes the pressure off and puts her at ease. You're also planting the idea in her head that you're not suggesting a coffee meeting because you're cheap; you're suggesting it because it's the perfect way to get to know her better without distractions. How can she argue with that? She can't—and she can't suggest the meal instead without sounding greedy and shallow either.

The danger, however, is that you lead the woman into thinking that she's not important to you and that you're the type of guy that dates around for sport. Obviously, this can end the relationship before you get what you want, so if she asks if you date often and you want to play it conservative, use this classic response from Johnny Shack:

> *Well yes, I do go out with a lot of girls because I'm picky.* She'll usually respond that it doesn't make sense that going out with a lot of girls means you're picky. Tell her that you go out with a lot of girls because you're still waiting to find the perfect girl. Then ask her if it is better to stay home alone, or to go out and search for the perfect woman. By framing the question this way you've forced her to respond, and any reasonable girl will have to admit that you're right—and, therefore, you must be the right man for her!

The Nickname Tease

A woman's curiosity is a wonderful tool. Use it. All the time. And any way you like. Keep her guessing. Keep her intrigued. Drop little teases and hints that you have to follow up on later.

A prime example of this is the nickname tease. When you're talking to your target on the phone, casually mention that you've thought of the best nickname for her—but don't tell her what it is. Make her beg for it; let her curiosity run wild. And then tell her that it's too personal to tell her over the phone, so you'd

The Perfect Nickname

It's smart to have a ready supply of nicknames that you can slip onto any girl. If you don't have a few favorites, though, and you're having trouble coming up with something juicy and romantic, try this trick:

1. Think of something sweet, yummy, or otherwise positive (sugar, butter, sparkle, soft, etc.).
2. Think of one part of her appearance that stands out from other women, or that she works to make stand out (lips, pants, eyes, cheeks).
3. Put the two words together, and you've got a romantic, endearing, and sexy nickname—Sugarlips, Butterpants, Sparkle-eyes, Softlips, etc..
4. Or maybe you don't. In which case, toss it out and start again. You'll come up with some that won't fly— Buttereyes, for example. Obviously, use your common sense to throw these out. Don't worry, once you've done this a few times, the process becomes very easy.

love to see her in person. Once you're together, it's your call when exactly you tell her the nickname, but don't be in a rush to tell her because (and yes it works!) she might be willing to make out with you or end up in bed with you just to find out her nickname.

Of course, you really do need to have a nickname for the girl. And make sure that it is sweet, endearing, romantic—and flattering! If she spends a lot of time and energy to find out the name, you want it to be something she's going to be grateful for. You want the nickname to push her into the bed, after all, not out the door. Nicknames usually will sound a bit silly to you, and you may feel self-conscious using them at first. Calling a woman "angel eyes" or "sugar lips" may sound totally stupid to you— it sounds stupid to me—but women eat this kind of thing up.

The nickname tease is perfect for any point in the relationship. It's also a great bridge if the woman isn't responding to your initial phone call like you want her to. For instance, say you've done all the right things and called up the next day. You expect her to be excited, as you suggested she be the night before. But she's not. In fact, she seems indifferent about going out with you. You need her in a state of drooling lust.

To get the woman into a state of lust, use intrigue to introduce the name to her. If you've gotten her curious about the "perfect nickname," she'll be thinking about the nickname—and about *you*. She decides "what the hell, I'll give it a try." Once she agrees to meet you in person, she's yours, my friend, because now you're able to work your magic on her again—eliciting values, becoming the man she wants and needs, negging her when necessary. And what woman can resist that game?

Intrigue is a valuable emotional state, because it gives the woman another excuse to see you. If she's on the fence, it will push her to your side; if she's into you already, it will make her that much more eager to please you. So don't ever be afraid to drop hints or make vague promises about how wonderful your afternoon together is going to be. It's a powerful aphrodisiac to be a man of mystery.

But remember: You must fulfill your promises and meet her expectations, or they'll boomerang back on you and she'll dump you for a man whose got the gift of words *and* actions.

The Meeting

The get-together (not date!) is no different than meeting the woman casually in a bar—you will be eliciting values, becoming the man of her dreams, getting kino, moving into sexual talk, and closing her with a kiss once again.

The difference is that, instead of having to approach her and break down her bitch shield, this encounter is going to start off at the "warm and friendly" stage. That's right, you're going to skip right past "polite and calm" and start this encounter halfway to

Advanced Kino Foot Action

One of the best moves you can use on a first get-together is the foot flirt. It's innocent, it's private, and it's something she can return without fear of social reprisal. So, if you're sitting at a table (the coffee shop again, for instance), touch her feet twice with your feet and see how she responds. Don't stomp, just kind of rub your foot up along hers and leave it there. Try to sync this kino with something positive in the conversation, but don't let it distract you from eliciting and demonstrating value.

If her response is ambiguous—in other words she isn't rubbing your ankle but she isn't pulling away either—touch her again and say, "Are you foot flirting with me?" in a joking way. Then touch her again. If she starts to respond, you're in.

home already. Otherwise, why even bother with the whole set-up?

Always arrive early, and if you're meeting her for coffee or at some other specific location, wait outside for her to arrive. When you see her, act enthusiastic. Hopefully, she will act enthusiastic when she sees you, not only because she's excited about meeting you but because you "told" her to be enthusiastic when you asked for her number, and then you reinforced that suggestion in the follow-up phone call.

Whether she's acting enthusiastic, however, doesn't really matter. Smile when you see her and give her a big hug right away. Take her hand and hold it all the way to wherever you're going to be settling in. And always watch her reaction! She's naturally going to be nervous about meeting you, but if you lead her with your actions you will actually see her go from nervous to happy, smiling, starry-eyed and glowing within a space of a few minutes.

Now is not the time for subtlety. Enthusiasm is contagious, so use it.

Inviting Her Over

You've had a great meeting; *you've kept it short and to the point*; and now it's time to move on to a romantic place to continue what you've started. The whole goal here, Sherlock, is to get her over to your place. It is not to have a good time and then tell her, "Thanks, I had a great time, let's do it again." That's a dating scenario, and you're not dating. But how do you invite a woman to your house? And when? Here are three different scenarios to walk you through the process:

Scenario 1

You're fluff talking and having a great time. You steer the conversation toward something that seems to hold her interest and which you know you have exhibits of at home—books, music, dogs, cats, movies, etc. Quite casually you mention, "You know, I have a great music collection at home." Soon after, you say, "Come to my place and check out the collection I was talking about." She turns you down.

What happened? You treated the meeting like an AFC. You were just fluff talking, not getting any real values. And then you tried a cheesy line, hoping the good time you were having was enough to get her to jump into your car. Well, it wasn't, because even though she was into you, she'd heard that line, delivered that way, a thousand times. You basically told her you were just another nobody in a long line of chumps.

Scenario 2

Fluff talk. Feelings talk. Demonstrate value and personality. You are making her feel good. She smiles, laughs, has a doggy-dinner-bowl look. You start some slight kino—touching hands, holding hands as you walk down the street. You know she likes music, so you say, "Come over to my place and see my new CDs." She agrees. You continue to work your magic back on your trusty sofa—making her feel good, relaxed, connected. Then it's time to show her that you want her to see more than just your CDs. She freezes from the shock and horror of the realization, then panics and flees.

What Happened? She came over to your place because she liked and trusted you. That's great—but it's not exactly the point, is it? Once you got back to your place, you had to push her to the point of realizing that you were after more than a tour of your CD collection. She was in an unfamiliar environment, she felt powerless, so you were basically pushing her toward running away. Okay, maybe she won't. Maybe she'll want to show you a little something, too. But there's no guarantee, and everything you've done has pushed her toward making a split second decision. She'll take the safe route and head out the door—*even if that's not what she really wants*.

Scenario 3

Fluff talk. Feelings talk. Demonstrate value and personality. She's feeling good, so you move on to slight kino. You touch her hand. She responds, so you continue on to more intimate kino: touching her hair, holding her waist, and finally the ultimate test, a kiss. You kiss for a while and then mention that you have some amazing CDs that, judging from your previous conversation, she should check out. She agrees, and you end up showing her far more than your record collection. You end up showing her a good time.

What happened? You used the same cheesy line as the first time, but this time everyone got what they came for. Why? Simply put, you didn't rush in for the score. You took your time and made sure that the reason you were inviting her to your house was perfectly clear. No surprises. When she excepted your invitation, she knew what that meant. And that's all because of the kiss.

The kiss is essential for two reasons:

1. Kissing is the ultimate test of her intentions. Kissing is a huge decision for a girl. This is fine, because in order to sleep with you she's going to have to make a huge decision on your worthiness at some point. Better to have her make it earlier in the evening, when she's comfortable, and have it be something that on the surface seems as "innocent" as a kiss. If she's reluctant to kiss you, she'll be reluctant to do anything more when she comes back to your place. Don't even invite her until she kisses you convincingly.

2. Kissing is a powerful aphrodisiac. She may have been thinking of coming and checking out your CD collection anyway, but now when she does it she's going to be horny. In fact, kiss her long enough, and she's liable to invite herself over—with less than pure intentions already in mind. In other words, you've got a girl that knows what to expect, and expects it.

So it's not the invitation that matters, it's the timing. If you're going to invite a girl—and there's no point in reading this book if that's not your intention—then you better kiss-test and arouse her first.

Dinner at Your Place

If you can kiss her and tongue her down, it's now time to invite her back to your place for the next "date." And the best way to do this is to cook for her.

Wait, I hear you. You don't want to actually spend any time or effort cooking (although if you do want to spend the time and effort, women love to see dominant men who can also cook). Prepared food that looks homemade is available at most grocery stores these days and makes a perfect meal for two. At most suburban grocery stores, you can buy a pre-roasted chicken or pre-marinated meat that you just throw in your oven, a salad in a bag, and even freshly made desserts, and in larger cities, spe-

A Dissenting Opinion

Of course, some PUAs are adamantly against even trying to invite the woman over to your place. Why risk having her slip out of the mood on the drive home, they ask. This is a valid point, and this kind of disappointment will occasionally occur. Still, I think inviting her home is the classy way to go and should always be your first option. If she doesn't want to wait for sex at your place, by all means fulfill her every fantasy, but only take this route if she indicates it first.

Still, I'm a fair guy, so I'll give the other side their chance. Here's NYC on the subject after someone tried to move a receptive girl to his place:

> Forget your house! If you had taken her somewhere secluded, you could have fucked her. . . . She was totally with it and you lost out because you tried to change the venue. . . . I personally don't like to change venues. Do her in the bathroom if you have to.

cialty stores will have pre-made meals that you can just heat up at home. If that doesn't work, make her some of your "special" spaghetti sauce from a jar, and just add a salad and a loaf of bread. Just don't serve her Hungry Man frozen dinners—and don't lie and say it's homemade if you got it pre-cooked from the grocery. The point isn't to impress her with the food; it's to get her to your place, fool.

The benefits of the meal at home "date" are numerous, beyond the fact that it's far cheaper than buying dinner anywhere else:

1. You're able to make the meal romantic with candles, music, and mood lighting.
2. Food is a sensual pleasure (oral gratification), and if you feed a woman she will associate that sensual feeling with

you. If you can literally feed something to her, the pleasure is that much greater. Some foods are better for this than others, so think about picking up a few strawberries, or better yet, chocolate covered strawberries, for dessert.

3. You've given yourself an air of competence and self-assurance. Women love feeling taken care of and provided for, and that's what serving them dinner does.

4. You've turned what would have been a public date into a private rendezvous in a place where you can go . . . right to bed, should she feel like it. And believe me, she will.

If She Has Second Thoughts

Ideally, once you've got the woman to your place and you've demonstrated value and laid on some heavy kino, the woman will simply have to have you. If you've done your homework, these instructions will work—most of the time. There are still times when the woman will object at the last possible moment, and then it's all up to you to make the right call.

First, you have to determine if she's serious or she's full of BS. Does she really not want to have sex with you? Or is she just worried about the repercussions?

I can't stress this enough: if she really doesn't want to have sex with you, *do not force the issue*! That is her prerogative, and it's your job to get her hot and bothered *before* it gets to the point of no return. Once she says no, you stop. Period. Never, even if you're convinced she wants what you've got, force yourself on a woman at all. That's rape, my friend, and they will lock you up for a long time.

However, that having been said, anything short of a "no" is still a negotiation. Many woman want to have sex with you, but when it comes time to perform they may hesitate for societal reasons. In that case, get her objections (she doesn't want to seem like a tramp, she's worried about diseases, etc.) and address them directly. Here are a few strategies:

Pattern Away Her Hesitation

If she's just "not sure" about going all the way, tell her that you understand and agree with her hesitancy, but you just can't help thinking about what a great time the two of you would have. You can even try this beauty from Ross Jeffries (www.seduction.com), perfect for any general objection: "We shouldn't do it, and we shouldn't enjoy it so much. And please don't try to convince me that you'd really want to do it. Now, with me, this is the way I see it . . ."

Society Sucks

Many women worry that, by having sex with you, they're being sluts or whores. That's not them talking, that's society screwing with their minds. You have to show them that society is wrong, and the best way to do that is to stack their realities and tell them stories, as in this example, again from Ross Jeffries (www.seduction.com):

> I just talked to my friend Tina about this, and she told me it is so unbelievably unfair that men can make love to any woman they choose, but if a woman wants to express her sexual liberty, she is frowned upon. And I completely agree with her, frowning is such an expression of utter hypocrisy.

Respect Her Objection

Many women have real hang-ups about being naked with men, especially the really gorgeous ones. It's hard to believe, I know, but it's true: even models often don't feel comfortable with their bodies in an intimate situation. So, be sensitive to her hesitancy and if she wants to do it with the lights off, do it with the lights off. It's not BS. In most cases, it's usually true, so respect those boundaries!

Counter Her Objection

If there's something holding her back, but you're not quite sure where it is, try this humorous approach:

Imagine I have a magic wand and I can use it to make anything you wish disappear. So just tell me one thing you'd
like me to make disappear in order for you to feel comfortable, because I hate to see you missing out on things you
should enjoy. It can be anything—a person, an attitude of
our society, something about yourself, something about me,
some other commitment you have—absolutely anything.
Now what would that one thing be?

There's a good chance that, having been forced to think
about her objection, it will seem small and insignificant already.
But don't count on that! Now that you know what's keeping her
from having the best experience of her life, eliminate that obstacle if you can.

The general idea is that you need to give her an excuse to
have sex with you. For many women, having sex with a virtual
stranger lowers their self-worth and self-esteem. They feel like
tramps, or that they're doing something wrong. You have to give
them a way around this personal objection. Or, as Jobet Claudio
calls it on Mindlist, you have to give them a Mental Escape Hatch.

It doesn't matter what this escape hatch is. She can blame
it on the wine, the music, the movie, the romance in the air: it
doesn't matter. Just give her an excuse and then let her do the
rest of the work.

The Mental Escape Hatch is just as important in post-fuck as
well. If she wakes up the next morning and starts giving you
excuses why she did it and saying that she'll never do it again . . .
don't argue with her! She's just trying to regain her self-esteem.
More often than not, the fact that she did the dirty with you one
time is enough of an excuse for her to do it with you again, no
matter what she says in the first light of morning.

It All Comes Down to Satisfaction

Women don't just want sex. They want great sex. As men, we're
usually just after any sex, but women are looking for great sexual
experiences. They will pass up a normal man, even an excep-
tionally good-looking man (or at least better looking than you)

for a man that sexually arouses them *and* promises, by his manner or image or personality, to be good in the sack.

Women want exciting, provocative, imaginative partners. Luckily for us, they're hard to find and most women are totally unfulfilled in their sexual life. The better looking a woman is, the more unfulfilled she probably is. Beautiful women—and I'm talking about the model-type beauties here—don't regularly get what they need or deserve. Instead, they get guys that cum too soon, fawn all over them, smother them, and then go bragging to their friends about the hot chick they bagged (and left totally unsatisfied).

Women's sexual desires are much greater than most men realize. And the better looking she is, the more likely she is to be used by guys for selfish sex. Never forget: you are the guy that is going to make her cum. You are the man that is going to deliver on the promise. Women know that good sex is hard to find—and once they have it, they will not let it go without a fight. That's right, *especially* the models.

I'm not going to give you sex lessons, but I will tell you two things:

1. *Pay attention to her*. Women want and need foreplay, and it will excite you and make the sex even better when it happens. While you are exciting a woman sexually, read her body and her reactions the way that you did when you were getting her into bed. Does she freeze up when you touch her nipples? Then move on—every woman has her own erogenous zones. Some women may get wet when you breathe gently on their necks, and some find the feeling just creepy. Read the woman's reactions, and you'll have her begging in no time.

2. *Practice makes perfect*. The more sex you have, the better you'll be. Your average sixteen-year-old boy takes about two minutes to have sex, which won't satisfy any woman. But, after a few partners, that same boy is a lot better—he takes longer and he has learned what satisfies a woman. Not only will you learn to delay your own orgasm, you'll make getting there a lot more fun for yourself and the woman.

CHAPTER **14**

The Relationship

<u>After Sex</u>

There are some of you that are reading this book because you're looking to seduce and impress a girl into a long-term relationship. Bravo for you! There are others of you that are simply after a one-night stand. Hey, I've been at that point in my life, too, so bravo to you as well!

If you're after sex and only sex, it's perfectly fine not to call the woman ever again after you've slept with her. In fact, it's better not to call her because you'll only be leading her on. If you don't want a relationship, make that clear *before* you bring her home, and then reinforce that idea by basically ignoring her from there on out.

If you want to continue the relationship, however, you must—and I mean absolutely *must*—call her the next day after having sex. It's a very, very big deal for a woman to give her body to you, so you must show her respect by calling her. If you don't call, she's going to feel hurt and used—and then she probably won't want to have sex with you ever again. Obviously, that's bad news for you.

But isn't calling her supplicating? Aren't you giving her the power? Won't that just turn her off? Not if you handle the relationship the PUA way, which is what this final chapter is all about.

Always Be Busy

Always let women know that you are an active person with a lot of things on your plate—even if it isn't true! If a woman thinks you're just sitting around all day, she'll either think you're a loser going nowhere or, worse, some desperate guy that's been rejected by every other woman on the planet.

If you imply that you're busy, on the other hand, she will think that you are a confident leader who knows what he wants and is going to get it. You will appear different from the other guys, all of whom are hanging off her begging for her time. You're not supplicating; you're showing her that she isn't your priority in life. You're making her do the chasing, and because of that you've put yourself above her in a place of control. She wants you more than you want her; therefore, you must be a catch. And besides, everyone wants what they can't have, right?

Never make a woman your first priority in life (unless, of course, you've found a woman you want a committed relationship with—the mother of your children or your wife *should* be your priority). Always put her second to something—family, career, friends, whatever—but leave her a small piece of hope that *if she's good enough* she can become number one. She may even suspect you have other women on the side. This is not a bad thing. She'll realize you're popular or, in other words, worth her time. And she'll try that much harder to use her charms to seduce you away from your other activities.

How do you make yourself appear busy? Here are a few quick tips adapted from the advice of Don "America's #1 Singles Expert" Diebel (www.getgirls.com):

- When a girl asks what you did yesterday, never say, "I just sat around and was bored." Better to say, "I was up early to run errands and take care of business, then

You're not going to be spending a lot of time with your "girl-friend" compared to the average clingy AFC, so to make scarcity effective you need to remember one thing: the time she spends with you must be absolutely amazing and without a doubt the best time she has with anyone. It's not the quantity, my friend, it's the quality, so always be ready to blow her mind.

played tennis, met a friend for lunch, and worked in the afternoon." Lie if you have to. And don't worry, you'll get used to it.

- If a girl calls and asks what you're doing, reply, "I just walked in the door," or "I'm just on my way out to take care of business."
- Don't hang on the phone for hours talking with women. Get the business of the call over with, be pleasant, then excuse yourself.
- Don't call a woman every day. Show her that you are busy and have other important things going on in your life. Let her know she has to compete for your time.
- If you run into a girl on the street, be pleasant and friendly. Show her that you're interested in her, then excuse yourself on an important errand. Before you go, be sure to set up a time to call her later that day, if possible. And then call her!

Suggest Competition

Chasing other women while in a relationship is perceived as cruel and insensitive. And it is—assuming you're in a traditional one-on-one relationship.

If you've established a traditional relationship with a girl and she hears you're chasing other girls, it's quite natural for her to assume that you are pursuing one-on-one relationships with them, thus abandoning her to be all alone. She will feel miserable, deceived, unhappy, and angry—and you are the cause of it all.

Have you been insensitive and cruel? Yes. For chasing other girls? No.

You are cruel because you have implied a one-on-one relationship, when, in fact, that was not your plan at all. You've been leading her in a false direction, and no amount of explaining after the fact will ease her anger or embarrassment. She will hate you for life—and so will her friends. And they are right to do so.

To avoid these nasty consequences, you have to define the relationship you want from the start. If you don't want to be with her exclusively, let her know. If she walks, well, she wasn't the right girl for you anyway. If she stays, you'll both get to enjoy the relationship on your terms. She won't have to feel paranoid, jealous, or nervous because she knows that, no matter how many other women you date, her position is secure. (But be warned, she will be paranoid and jealous, nonetheless. That's just how women are when there's competition around.) Plus, in this kind of relationship, she's free to pursue her own interests without guilt or shame. Don't tell her this, though. You don't particularly want her having hot sex with other guys (unless you're invited) and besides, it sounds too much like an AFC-style dumping.

It's best not to lie to get a woman in the sack; however, it's best not to be too flagrant about your womanizing habits until after you've shown her what she'll be missing if she walks away. So be honest, but be discreet. Tell her you are already engaged in a few other sexual relationships, that those women understand that you are not monogamous right now, and that you hope she can accept that too and learn to love your time together, because quality time together is what it's all about.

If she accepts your terms, show her the time of her life—but always drop reminders of your single status. Have the names and numbers of other girls popping out of your wallet or leave them lying around your house, apartment, or car. Don't be desperate for her, and don't be available at all times. Obviously, the

---

Advice from a Player

I consulted a real lady's man (alphahot1, ASF) for some player advice. His experience suggests a guy should handle only three women at once. Not all at once (although that happens too), but over time. That means keeping five or six women going at all times: three in "active" mode and two or three in the wings. If a woman starts to get out of line, dump her immediately and replace her, always keeping the number of women on the string about the same.

This arrangement basically guarantees that you will get laid every night, if that is your goal. And because you're not stretching yourself thin, you can still have a life outside of sex and seduction (if you want that kind of thing).

---

best and most fun way to accomplish this is to have five women going on the side.

Finally, feel free to be erratic in your behavior. Call her up and ask her to meet you in an hour. Show her a whirlwind fabulous time, followed by an insane hour of romance, then don't call her for four days. That's the best way to keep a woman on her toes and avoid being taken for granted.

Put a Price on Yourself

"Make her put some work into hanging out with you in order for her to value you. Make her come and pick you up, make her spend some money on you, make her call you and do you favors. When she does things for you it will justify her own feelings for you."

—Craig, *Clifford's Seduction Newsletter*

Confidence works two ways. You have to have the confidence to go for what you want, and the confidence to leave behind what you don't need. If a woman doesn't value you and your company, then you must have the confidence to leave her behind. And how do you know if she values you? You make her pay to be with you.

One of the most powerful realities of human nature is that if something comes at very little cost, people assume it has little value. In other words, if it's free, people assume it's junk. They confuse price with value, and often they don't take the time to find out the real value of the object they've left behind.

In other words, you'd better cost something or the woman isn't going to think you're worth anything. And I'm not talking about money here, although having her pay for your dinner occasionally is a great way to demonstrate value and keep the relationship in your control. You've got to make her personally invest in you, and struggle to overcome obstacles. Here are a few practical ways to do that, courtesy of Ross Jeffries (www.seduction.com):

- Show your anger. Guys who never get mad, who never show a woman that they can stand up for themselves, are giving themselves away for free. Never hit a woman or berate her. But if she crosses the line, you have to tell her you won't accept that kind of behavior.

- Be willing to be unavailable. That which is scarce is clearly more valuable, right? That's why diamonds are worth more than rocks. So, be a diamond.

- Occasionally cancel dates and make her call you twice before returning her call. Don't make a habit of it, but every now and again show her you're not her toy on a string.

Judge Her by Her Actions, Not Her Words

Many women are excellent excuse makers and bamboozlers. They make promises they don't keep. They break dates. They don't call. In short, they show you disrespect . . . all the time.

AFCs will ignore these signs of trouble and keep hanging on, focusing on the positives. They try to show their appreciation of and interest in a woman, rather than get her respect, which is why, like Rodney Dangerfield, they don't get any!

A PUA, on the other hand, is always focused on how he is being treated. Each move he makes is put through the test: "Will this increase or decrease the priority she gives me?" And then, once the action is taken, he judges her reaction. If he's being treated with respect, then he'll focus on the positives. If he's not, he'll change tactics and put her in her place—or drop her like a hot potato.

In the next few sections, I'll look at a few important trouble signs, and how to deal with them.

If She Disrespects You

It's very important to set the rules early in a relationship. Don't whine or get mad, but make it very clear where your boundaries are and what isn't acceptable. If she complies with your rules, then great. She'll receive the best time of her life in return. If she breaks them, well, you have to call her on it.

Disrespect is a test. She is trying to find out whether you are a supplicating groveling AFC or a real man. In order to pass such a test, you must:

1. Never lose your temper.
2. Never whine like a baby.
3. Show her that her behavior doesn't really faze you.
4. Show her that you find her behavior disrespectful and that you don't need to tolerate it.

The fourth step is the most important. Women will always test your limits, so you can't be afraid to call them on their bullshit. Tell them you won't put up with it and not to do it again. If she does it again, dump her. There are millions of women out there, so good riddance.

The Returning Fox Theory

Often, when you've dumped a disrespecting girl and shown her you're a real man, she will suddenly want to get back together with you. Don't let her back in so easily. Tell her in no uncertain terms that her behavior was unacceptable, and that the only way she's going to get back with you is if she does something really special. It can be anything you want— use your imagination—she broke the rules, so now she has to make it up to you. The point is that she's crawling back, so now you have the power. If she doesn't want to make it up to you, send her packing. She was never the girl for you anyway.

This is called The Returning Fox Theory. The Returning Fox works for disrespectful women, women who have returned to your life after you've forgotten about them, or even those who have ignored you at a club or party and then returned later to talk with you.

And while you're free to ask whatever you want of a Returning Fox, one word of caution: only use sex as a condition in extreme situations. It is an aggressive strategy that's more likely to make you look like a horny jerk than to actually get you some satisfaction. Try something a little more subtle instead.

If She Doesn't Return Your Phone Calls

If she isn't returning phone calls, things are looking pretty grim. But not all is lost if you've mastered the ways of the PUA.

Your first option, of course, is to call her or E-mail her some more, saying that you are confused as to why she hasn't answered but it's OK, let's try again. This is the perfect approach . . . if you want to lose the girl and your self-esteem.

Your second option is to not respond at all. You called her. She got the message. Now the ball is in her court. This method allows you to keep your integrity and pride, but it also means you usually lose the girl. But she wasn't interested anyway, right? Not necessarily. She could have just been taking a while to make up her mind, or maybe she's the kind of girl that likes to take a few orders from a real man before giving in.

So, if you have high hopes—you hit it off, the "date" went well, the sex was spectacular—you've got to show her you will not tolerate this behavior if you're going to win her back. Give her one more chance because you saw so much potential in the relationship:

> Hi. This is [your name]. I wanted to let you know how disappointed I was that you didn't call me back. But, since I saw so much potential for us I thought I would give you one last chance. So why don't you give me a call.

Or, even better, give her one last opportunity to seize the day and have the time of her life:

> Hi. So are you going to make time to meet me and have the time of your life, or are you always busy? I'm free on Sunday afternoon.

If she doesn't respond, move on without looking back.

If She Cancels a Date Without Notice

In my opinion, you should dump her. Right there. If she's a good girl, she'll become your Returning Fox, especially if she was testing you, and had no real excuse. If not, she's not for you anyway. Of course, this is rather extreme. So if you want to give her another chance, try this routine from Ross Jeffries (www.seduction.com):

Her: I can't make it. I've got a rare tropical disease that's causing me to shrink by the hour.
You: *(silent for as long as it takes her to talk again)*
Her: Hello? Are you there? What's wrong?
You: What's wrong is I can't believe the bullshit I'm hearing.
Her: What?

You: Look . . . you made a commitment to spend time with me and now you're blowing me off. You're disrespecting me and my time, and I'm not going to put up with it. My rule is, if someone makes a commitment to me, I expect them to keep it. If they can't keep it, I need to know at least a day in advance so I can make other plans. Got it? If you can live with that rule, great. If not, sayonara.

Then, hang up. Does this work? You better believe it does! In most cases, even with the most jaded women, you'll get a call back in five minutes asking you on a date.

If She Keeps You Waiting

Some women will keep you waiting outside in your car for ten minutes when you come by to pick them up. Other women will invite you in, then ignore you while they talk on the phone or do something else totally unrelated. This may seem like a small thing, but you should know by now that even the small things are totally unacceptable. So, if this happens to you, try this routine, again from Ross Jeffries (www.seduction.com):

You: Can I ask you a question?
Her: Sure.
You: Are you being intentionally rude to test me, or are you just an accidental asshole?
Her: *(mouth dropping open in shock)*
You: Don't ever keep me waiting like this again, okay? I'll always treat you with respect, but I expect the same. Do you understand?
Her: Uh . . . uh . . . yes.
You: Good. Let's see you make it up to me.

At this point, grab her and kiss her passionately. If you can, turn this into sex then and there. Why give her an evening on the town (splitting the costs, of course) and reward her rotten behavior?

If She LJBFs You

Ideally, you should never get to the point where a girl says, "Let's just be friends." This should only happen to AFCs, because it means that she's not interested in you and you haven't taken the hint. PUAs should be able to make any woman who's willing to spend time with them also be interested in them sexually. If it's not working out, you need to cut and run first, before she negs you and makes you feel like a chump.

If you wind up in this situation, however, the choice is clear. Tell her: "No, I have lots of friends. See you later." This has been known to turn the relationship around, but don't count on it. You've let her get to the LJBF zone, so you have no respect from her, sucker.

If you're still interested in the girl for some reason (not recommended), then completely cut off contact with her for at least two months. When you come back, you can basically start from scratch seducing her all over again, without having to fear that she still is thinking of you as—yuck!—a friend.

The Power of (Her) Friends

Of course, a relationship—even a non-exclusive relationship—isn't all about having the power and being in control. You've also got to be the man of her dreams, at least in the few hours a week you spend with her, so you'd better be showing her a good time.

The easiest way to get on her good side is to impress her in front of her friends. Always show her friends (as opposed to telling them) that you are a good guy. Be friendly and flirty with them, and go out of your way to treat them right. Never underestimate a girl's desire to make her friends jealous of her man. If her friends like you—or even better, want you—then you've risen that much higher in her eyes. If they hate you, it's only a matter of time before the relationship sours.

Don't misunderstand me: if they like you but think you're wrong for her, especially if they think you're too much of a player, this can actually work to your advantage. So be smooth and flirty, but always be polite.

If you really want to play the friend card, go ahead and comment to your girl how attractive her friends are. If she thinks you might be interested in one of them, she'll work that much harder to keep you. Or you can go the other way and say that your girl is much better looking than all her friends. That's a confidence boost right there, and one that will endear you to her even more.

Aren't friends wonderful!

Reveal Secrets

Reveal secrets. But reveal them slowly! Women like a man of mystery, but they love to learn a secret or two about you. This is a great way to establish rapport . . . if you don't take it too far, too fast. Women like the idea of peeling away layers. They want to learn a little bit more about you, to have you reveal yourself slowly, but they always want to believe there is more to find out. If a woman thinks she knows you, she'll get bored. So, convey the image that you have a lot of secrets, and that you're willing to reveal them periodically—for the right price!

Pay Compliments

Compliments are relationship currency, so treat them with respect.

If she compliments you? Don't be an ignorant bum, thank her. Say, "How nice of you to say that. You are very sweet." Don't play modest and fend it off, and don't act ungrateful and self-servingly declare, "Darn right. It's about time you noticed." Just make her feel good about having complimented you.

Complimenting her. Complimenting a girl is a double-edged sword. Some girls will hang on to a guy that compliments them just for the positive reinforcement; others will dismiss a guy that pays them compliments as just another chump. So always know your girl, and know her values, before you attempt to compliment her.

Even with the compliment-haters, it is worthwhile to compliment her occasionally. But you can never be hesitant or bland. If you can't make the compliment sincerely passionate and unique, it's best not to say anything at all. But if you *can* make it passionate and unique, you can get even that jaded, dismissive girl to fall into your arms with a loving sigh. So always remember these simple rules of complimenting:

1. Don't compliment the obvious. She knows about the obvious, she's heard those compliments before. She's just going to associate you with the loser AFCs that supplicated to her with the same compliments and got nowhere.

2. Do compliment things that aren't obvious, and make sure to explain what it is you like about it. This shows that you're thoughtful and perceptive, unlike those chumps that have drooled over her most obvious assets. If you describe how her wonderful trait makes you feel, she'll be feeling that positive emotion right along with you.

Always remember that compliments linger in the mind. In other words, she will think of the compliment again. If it's the right compliment, as defined above, she will remember you in an affectionate manner. If it's the wrong compliment, she'll keep thinking of you as a chump. So *only* pay her the right compliments.

Never compliment a woman on her body until you know her (unless you're going GM style, of course). But once you know her and have been with her, compliment the parts of her body you like and she'll adore you for it. Most women crave body compliments more than personality compliments, so use them. Just follow the rules above, and don't rush to comment like the horny pervert you are.

If I Said You Had a Beautiful Body...

It makes me uncomfortable if a guy comments on my body in any way, as in "You look good in that skirt." That's way too familiar for just meeting someone. It's too obvious that they're trying to pick me up.

—Karen, St. Paul

Romance, Romance, Romance

Sometimes it's good to drop the "I'm an uncontrollable bad boy" act and communicate something special to her. That's right, every relationship needs a little romance, even if you're a player. You can switch back to your no-supplication mode later, but just remember what Jennifer Lopez said: "I want a tough guy with a heart of gold." She may not be the brightest bulb in the basket, but she definitely knows what beautiful women want.

Here's a few romantic ideas, for use only with women you have already proven their love for you!

- Send or read her a poem.
- Send her an e-card, such as those from www. bluemountain.com. It's free and easy and women go gaga over them.
- Buy her a special little gift, but don't spend much money on it. You are much better off buying her something cheap, such as a twenty-five cent plastic ring, and then explaining to her why it has special significance for your relationship. This shows you're not buying her love with money, but thoughtfulness.
- Hide the present somewhere she'll find it—in the pocket of her coat, in her purse, under her pillow—but some-place she'd never expect to find a memento from you.

- Tell her you'll be late, then show up early and take her to dinner. Since you never pay for dinner for her, this is a rare treat that will be appreciated.
- Write her a letter (a real letter, not an E-mail) and leave it next to her pillow.
- Cook a special dinner for her.
- Take a long walk in the park together. Plan a trip to the zoo or a boat ride.
- Read something romantic or erotic together.
- Take her someplace for the weekend that she's always wanted to go, but never had time for. Surprise her with the trip.

Finally, always act and speak as if you two have something special going on that can't be found anywhere else. Don't just tell her that, because she may (God forbid) disagree. Tell her how happy you are that you have such a special relationship and elaborate on those feelings until she's nodding and smiling along. This is the best gift you can give her (and yourself), and it's absolutely totally free!

And Finally . . .

You should always remember that a woman can only experience real passion if she believes, on some level, that she could lose you.

This is true in all facets of life. If you hold something too tight, if you refuse to let go, then you become dependent. If that something is a person, he or she will cease to value you. Why bother, they think? You obviously need them more than they need you.

If you've seen a woman who was interested in you suddenly walk away as if you were nothing, this was probably the reason. If you've seen a red-hot relationship grow ice-cold, this is probably the cause.

For the Hot and Heavy Relationship

Here are a few tips from Don "America's #1 Singles Expert" Diebel (www.getgirls.com) to be used in the event the relationship is getting a little serious.

- Name a star in the universe for her. The International Star Registry will send her a 12 x 16-inch parchment (no more than thirty-five letters) and two sky charts showing its position in the galaxy, suitable for framing.

- Send her a telegram (Yes, a telegram!) telling her how much you care about her.

- Give her a newspaper published on her birthday or on the date of an important event in your relationship. Original newspapers from more than fifty cities are available, dating back to 1880 from Newspaper Archives.

- Buy an erasable marker and write something sweet on her windshield. Put a few paper towels under her windshield wiper so she can wipe it off.

- Write her a romantic letter, and then casually ask her to proofread your work.

- Take her on a romantic picnic. Bring a blanket, food, flowers, and champagne on ice.

- Buy her a helium-filled balloon and mail it to her. This will be a totally unexpected surprise.

- And last, but not least, buy her flowers. They never fail to make a lasting impression.

You must always be willing to walk away in life: from a seduction situation, from a one-night stand, from a relationship, even from a job. You are the prize to be pursued. You are a person of value. You are the opportunity of a lifetime *for them*, and if they aren't prepared to value that opportunity, then they don't deserve to have it.

There are a thousand other fish in the sea, and, as of now, you can catch every one of them. So, happy fishing, my friend!

Acknowledgments

In my exhaustive (and sometimes exhausting) search for knowledge, I have taken advice from literally thousands of PUAs the world over. I cannot thank or acknowledge them all, but I'd like to take a moment to recognize a few I consider the best of the best. These PUAs were my mentors when I was trying to be more than just another AFC, and you will find their wisdom, most of the time filtered through my own experiences but sometimes quoted directly, scattered throughout this book.

Don Diebel. The original PUA, Don's advice dates from the 1970s and the first sexual revolution. No PUA can do without some of Don's "golden oldies." If you would like more free dating tips on how to successfully meet, date, attract, and become intimate with women, please visit his website, www. getgirls.com.

Ross Jeffries. The creator of a seduction technique based on NLP (NeuroLinguistic Programming) called Speed Seduction®. Speed Seduction® is probably the most important breakthrough in seduction in the last two decades. You will find a summary of his techniques in the section on patterning (p. 125). All material from Ross Jeffries is copyrighted 1994 and 2003, Ross Jeffries, and used with permission. His website is www.seduction.com.

Maniac High. A Tokyo-based PUA. Maniac's articulate web advice more than anything else taught me the value of confidence and control. You can hear directly from Maniac at his website: www.pickupguide.com.

Mystery. A Los Angeles-based PUA and outspoken proponent of neg hits (p. 89), the best technique ever devised for scoring those model-beautiful women you thought were forever out of your reach. Guess what: they're not.

NYC. A New York-based PUA, and probably one of the greatest PUAs on the planet today, whose advocacy of eliciting values finally helped me bridge the gap between making a good impression and closing the deal.

Nathan Szilard. A Paris-based PUA and advocate of the GM technique (p. 80). Not my personal favorite, but if you have the right personality, definitely worth your time.

I would also like to thank ASF posters **Anubis**, **Nightshadow**, **James L. King, III**, and **Ray Parker**.

For information on the Web, I highly recommend the usenet group alt.seduction.fast (ASF for short), which was founded by Ross Jeffries and has since become a veritable encyclopedia of seduction advice. Of course, being a usenet group, it is also cluttered up with terrible advice, irrelevant insight, and general stupidity. This book in some ways started as an attempt to make the great information in ASF easy to find and follow, and then grew from there. I want to extend a special thank you to all my fellow regulars on this page, especially those I've quoted in this book!

Other outstanding sources of information and tips I highly recommend are Mindlist (www.egroups.com/group/mindlist), *Clifford's Seduction Newsletter*, *Sweep Women off Their Feet and into Your Bed*, www.showgirls.com, and the *Maxim* magazine advice pages at Maxim.com, the best source for the female perspective on dating and seduction.

And, of course, don't forget to visit my site, www.layguide.com, the Bible of online seduction tips. See you there!